C000313084

THE WITCH DOCTOR'S GUIDE TO SERVICENOW

Knowledge is around to be shared, not to be forgotten.

By Göran Lundqvist

Copyright © 2019 Göran Lundqvist
All rights reserved.

Special thanks to:

I will of course like to send a huge thanks to my family of Åza, Lovisa & Isaac. Without their acceptance, I would never been able to write this book. It has been many late hours and sitting at the computer instead of doing things with the family.

I like to thank all of those who have contributed to this book by answers community posts, writing blog posts, making videos or just answering my own questions when I have approached them. I don't take credit for all the ideas and functionalities that appears in the book, I just try to make sure that as many as possible get to learn all the great things you can do with ServiceNow.

And of course I can make this list go on for a very long time, but I would especially like to thank Tim Woodruff pushed me into the path of doing this and being there with all my questions about Kindle, book writing and Dave Spangler for keeping up with me and reviewing the whole book.

Disclaimer

The author of this book is not an employee or representative of ServiceNow. The content is entirely the author's own. This book has not been reviewed, approved, or endorsed by ServiceNow.

Contents

4

WHO AM I?

My name is Göran Lundqvist and I work as a consultant within the ServiceNow world. I have been working with IT through my whole life and my journey began when I was nine. I got my Commodore 64 and discovered how to start programming in Basic and hacking games on the beloved cassette tapes. For those who been there, long live "Turbo".

I have always been a happy gamer/geek and heading down the path of Dungeons & Dragons to discover its secrets. I went to schools in computer science, when it was finally time to graduate to become a technical project leader for building big WAN networks and intelligent houses the IT bubble burst. So instead, I ended up in a Help Desk. From there I have travelled down a road with many twists and turns. I have taken on many roles; including team manager, third line technical support, process owner and system administrator.

Around 2014 my old employer decided to change to ServiceNow and for me it was love at first sight. All the things that took so long to do in the old system suddenly became so simple. One of the first things I did was join the community and start looking at what other questions people had and what answers they provided. I really delved into all of this to learn everything I could and find out about ServiceNow.

After a year, I felt that I now could start helping others with answers instead of just asking questions. The appreciation of the members when I managed to help pushed me to contribute even more. From there on my journey really took off, I started my own blog where I posted things I found and how to solve the problems I ran into. I soon after connected to the ServiceNow Advocate program and started to blog for the community, which was even more fun.

In 2017, ServiceNow chose me to join the ranks of the ServiceNow MVP Class of 2017 and later as well for the class of 2018 & 2019 for which I am humbled and proud of.

Finally, I am a big performance/best practice junkie and really want to tweak ServiceNow to get every bit of performance from it that I can manage (as long as it is done the right way of course).

WHY AM I WRITING THIS BOOK?

I have been thinking a lot of writing this book. Ever since I was a technical reviewer of another ServiceNow book, I could not shake the feeling that I should write my own book. A question that kept coming back was "If I could travel back to when I started out with ServiceNow, what kind of advice would I want to give to myself?"

Well, after I started out as a customer in 2014 and seeing ServiceNow for the first time to where I am now; there has been many "Aha" moments and banging my head into the wall and as we all know, one of the best things about ServiceNow is that you can pretty much do anything.

As you all know, the bad part about it is that anything you want to do, you can usually solve in at least three different ways and not all ways are good. Some can generate real performance issues or be hard to maintain.

We all think in the start we have done it the best way, but after more experience and knowledge; you realized that solving it through that Client Script with some nasty code might not been the best way.

Therefore, I am writing this book to help all the people not to make the same mistakes I did. So, treat this book as a guide on your personal journey. I have included most of the information & knowledge I gathered since I started with ServiceNow. Looking back, I can honestly say that I would have done many configurations and customizations very differently knowing what I know now.

However, it sums up to the simple "knowledge is power" and when you are given an assignment you solve it with the knowledge you have at that given time. Nothing more, nothing less. Then it is up to you to keep learning, evolve and make it better. Who knows, I might be reading your book in a few years?

When it comes to Knowledge is power, I am a strong believer of sharing. The path forward has no room for trying to keep the knowledge for yourself. There will be so much knowledge and the flow will keep in a pace that is incredibly strong. If we are supposed to keep up, maintain and make it a better place, we need to share what we know and learn what others know.

WHO IS THIS BOOK FOR?

This book is mainly for people with a ServiceNow admin/developer/architect role. People who wants to get a power surge of "nice to know" stuff, to get a good understanding on how some of the fundamental platform functionality works and how to get it to work as good as possible.

To get maximum out from the book, it requires that you have worked in ServiceNow before and know the basics and the ServiceNow vocabulary. Nothing stops you from reading it now and after a while, going back to get the last pieces that might not have made sense the first time you read it.

I have gathered all this information from my ServiceNow years. Many of the examples and information are from sources from the internet, both official and unofficial ServiceNow places but even if all the things are fact based, it is still my own personal opinion, thoughts and guidelines that I use when I work with ServiceNow.

In this book, there are different examples. Many of these I have investigated, stumbled over or created myself to overcome a specific requirement. Some of these you can probably just take right away and reuse, and some might need some tweaking just give you an idea how to solve certain requirements and you create the solution by yourself.

The examples in the book gives a brief description on how the requirement might be but are broken down from where the implementation occurred in the system. All the examples are working in the Madrid release and most of the examples can be find within the GitHub Repository: https://github.com/goranlundqvist/The-Witch-Doctors-Guide-To-ServiceNow

HOW TO BECOME AN MVP

People ask me what they should do to become an MVP. The answer is not an easy one. For me, I have always been looking at those Microsoft MVP people and wondering how they got there. I also saw how active they were on helping others, sharing the knowledge they have.

I would say that this is the foundation and you need to have the urge to help others and share. Then you need to be ready for the amount of time it takes. For me, it is more of a passion and hobby. I love working with ServiceNow, finding solutions on complex problems and helping others.

I have no problem sitting a few hours at the community, helping instead of watching some movies or playing some games on the mobile. I still love sitting down and playing Xbox a whole evening; we all need to relax sometime. The only difference is that I just do not do it as often as before.

For ServiceNow, which is such a huge platform, if you want to reach MVP, you need to spend a lot of time to achieve it. It is just like anything else that you want to be good at, work hard. You will not be in the elite league in CS: GO or playing in NHL if you do not put all your blood, sweat and tears into it.

In the end, it is still up to ServiceNow to decide who should be in MVP class. You can only do your best and hope that you will make it. If you do not make it, work even harder for the next year's class.

If you do get into the MVP Class, acknowledge your achievement, but understand that you still need to work even harder if you want to maintain it and be in the next year's MVP Class.

WORKING IN SERVICENOW

Before going into any more practical examples, I would like to spend a few words about general guidelines that you can have in the back of your head. No matter if it's a new requirement or troubleshooting a bug, there are some places and guidelines I usually follow. These are mainly based on that I have done all the mistakes myself and hopefully I can help you down the road and avoid at least some of the mistakes I made.

When you get requirement from the business about functionality that they want within ServiceNow, I always follow these bullet points to be as prepared as I can.

- **Baseline functionality that you want to activate/use for the first time:** Always go to docs first and see what it says about the functionality. Even if you read it for an older release, there might be new functionality, or it might even be deprecated. It also might have a different configuration than when you last read about it.

- **Functionality that you don't know exists:** Don't throw yourself to start building it from scratch. Often, I see on the community people asking questions about a solution they made and having problem with that can instead been replaced with Baseline functionality straight off, or just with a little tweaking.

- **Plugins:** Another place to look is also the plugins in ServiceNow. There is a specific module for these that looks like this:

As you can see, it looks a bit different default in the Madrid release. I really like the newer look and it's easier to find and read about a plugin. You can always go back to the list as well if you want to do that. Here you can see which plugins exists and which ones are already activated. For almost all plugins there is also a link to the documentation site for you to read more about it. Also remember that some functionality might be activated or inactive depending on if it's a fresh installation for a specific release or the instance has been upgraded to that release.

Better security around local admins

Many clients are using local admin accounts to handle both administration and development in all their instances. If this is something that is used in your organization, I would recommend turning on the multifactor authentication to harden the security for these accounts. This means that when you are logging on as an admin, you will need to both provide your local password and a passcode from the google authenticator app that exists for both android and iOS phones. You can also configure it to send an email with a passcode if you google authenticator doesn't work or isn't available.

Depending on what release you are on, you might need to activate the plugin, but from fresh install from Kingston release, it should come activated in the Baseline Configuration. The plugin you are looking for is called **Integration – Multifactor Authentication**.

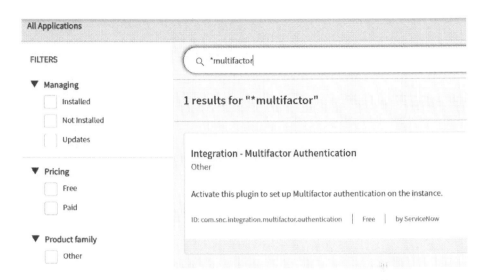

After that has been activated, you are basically just a few steps from having it up and running. There are a few properties which can be found in the application navigator under "Multi-factor Authentication->Properties".

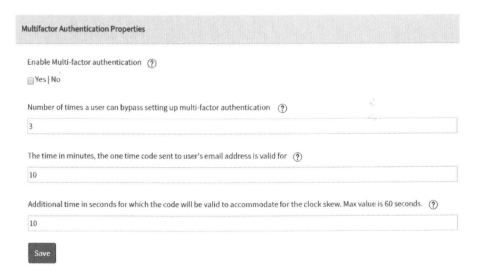

In these properties, you can activate the functionality for the whole instance. This needs to be activated for you to setup the functionality for the users. You can also set how many times a user can choose not to use it and so on.

Now, to turn it on for a user is very simple. There is a field on the user table called **Enable Multifactor Authentication** and default it's set to false. In the baseline form it might not be visible, so you need to add it yourself if you want easy access to set the value. Checking this box will force the user to use the Multifactor login.

User	
Abel Tuter	

User ID	abel.tuter
First name	Abel
Last name	Tuter
Title	
Department	Product Management
Password	
Password needs reset	☐
Locked out	☐
Active	✔
Enable Multifactor Authentication	☐

Now, recommended is that making this process as automated as possible, so e.g. a user is added to a specific group, in this example the admin-group, it will automatically get the field set to true.

After this quick configuration it's ready to work. First time you try to login to your instance, it will demand that you setup the app with you instance & account. And then it works.

Now you have strengthened your admin account so it's a lot harder for someone to take over the control of it and make a mayhem in your instance.

Short cuts through the application navigator

After you have been working with ServiceNow for a while you will start to learn the tables name instead of its label. For example, Change is change_request and Request is sc_request. Now, when you know this, you can start using a quick and simple short cut to get to 3 different things:

- **.list:** if you add .list to the end of the table name it will take you to a list view of all the records that exists within that table. Example: change_request.list

- **.form:** if you add .do to the end of the table name you will be taken to the form of a new record within that table. Example: change_request.form

- **.config:** if you add .do to the end of the table name you will be taken to an overview of all the configurable things for that table. Example: change_request.config. This is the same view you get if you on a form go to the context menu and choose "Configure->All".
  Note: This functionality came with the Jakarta release and won't work on earlier releases.

Depending if you write for example .list with lower or upper case will give either give you the new list in the same tab (lower case) or in a new tab (upper case). I find this very useful and I use this often to open new things in a new tab to keep what I'm working on in the current context frame.

Keyboard short cuts in the application navigator filter

Sometimes there is a lot of modules in your application navigator that even if you start typing the name of the module, you still will get too many results. For example, if you want to find client scripts and starts to type client, your wanted result is way down in the list. But if you instead type **ent sc** you will see that the result gets down to only a few results and client scripts is one of them. So how did that work? What we did was to take the last letters in the first word cli(ent) and the two first in the second word (sc)ripts. A lot less modules were matching this filter.

Here are a few examples to make your day to day business easier:

Application/Module:	Short cut:
User administration	er ad
Business rules	s r
Client scripts	s r
Script include	pt i
My work	y w
Scheduled jobs	d j

Then it will work like this:

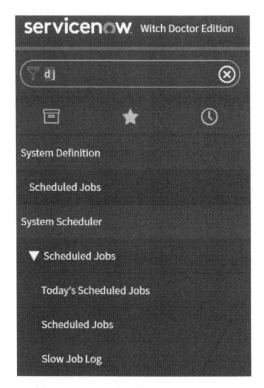

Another way you can actually do is not starting to type the first letter that a module/application starts with, but choose a combination anywhere in the words. E.g. you can type "yt" and the first Baseline application you will get is "Performance Anal(yt)ics.

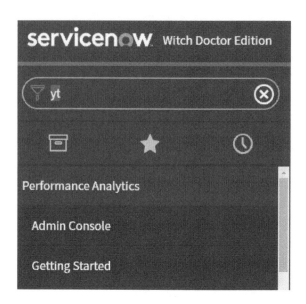

Syntax Editor Macros

These macros are pretty much a hidden gem and I hardly see people use them. But when you started to understand what they are for and how your life as an admin/developer is simplified, you never want to go somewhere without them.

You can find the Syntax Editor macros here:

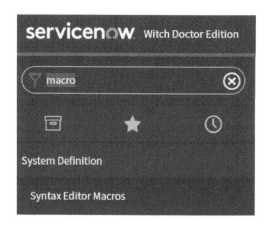

As you probably have noticed, much of the code that you write is repeatable and are the same over and over again in different places. Now these macros are here to make your life a lot easier. There are a few Baseline and you can easily add your own. Just remember that the macros you create aren't personal, everyone on the instance who have credentials to edit a script editor, will be able to use the macros. So, what do they do? If we look at the Baseline ones there is for example a macro called vargr.

If you type vargr and press "TAB" in a script editor, this will replace "vargr" with the code that is inside the field "text" in the macro record.

For this example, it will output:

```
var gr = new GlideRecord("$0");
gr.addQuery("name", "value");
gr.query();

if (gr.next()){
}
```

You won't see the $0. This was a variable for the script to know where to put the marker, but this doesn't work anymore.

If you type **help** and press **TAB** in the script editor you will see a list over every macro there is to use and as well the text that is in the comment field on each macro. Like this:

The Syntax Editor macros are:

----

doc - Documentation Header
for - Standard loop for arrays
vargror - Example GlideRecord Or Query
info -
method - Standard JavaScript Class Method
vargr - A common pattern of creating and querying a GlideRecord

As you can see there isn't any text after "info" and that is because there isn't any text in comment field on that macro.

Good to know as well that these macros only work in a script editor field, so it won't work in e.g. scripts – background.

System properties

System properties is a great functionality to store configuration settings that are used within the instance. Often, it's told to use this to hold values instead of e.g. hardcoding a sys_id in the code of a business rule. Since it's easier to administrate and doesn't require an update of the code when you just want to change the value. This can then easily be done in the system property instead of the business rule code.

But, and there is of course times when you shouldn't do like this either. If you change a system property too often, you can run into performance issues.

So when are you going to use system properties as a solution for your configuration? The answer is when storing configuration data that rarely or never changes its value. A good example would be that if a system property is changing its value more than once a month, then it shouldn't be stored as a system property but instead in a custom table that holds the configuration.

The reason behind it all is how ServiceNow handles changes on system properties. When you change a system property, ServiceNow flushes the cache on all nodes to make sure that all the nodes in the cluster are in sync (having the same system properties). Doing this can have a huge effect on the performance for 1-10 minutes when it actually rebuilds the whole cache and it's while the cache is rebuilding the degradation in performance occurs. When the cache is flushed, all the queries instead goes to the database which can result in: higher CPU usages in both the database servers and the application nods and higher response times. This means that changing a system property has the same effect as writing cache.do in the URI like **https://<INSTANCE_NAME>.servicenow.com/cache.do**. And I had no clue as a fresh developer that changing a system property like that could have that huge effect on the systems performance.

Sometimes you read about a specific system property that either someone has suggested for a solution on e.g. the community or even specified in the documentation site. Then you go to your instance and into system properties and there you will notice that it doesn't exist. Don't be alarmed of this. Not all system properties exist as a record in the instance from baseline. Some of the properties needs to be created by you and it isn't a big deal. Just make sure you enter the correct name and value and it will work as a charm.

Useful properties

Here are some properties that I have stumbled across and they have help me solved some issues/functionalities that I have had.

- **glide.ui.ui15_switch_roles:** Defines on who can switch between UI15 and UI16. This holds the roles that the user needs to have to be able to see the button. In the Baseline, this property doesn't exist, and it means that only the users with admin role will see the button.

- **glide.ui.list_mechanic.roles:** This handle which users are allowed to personalize a list view. It contains a list with roles which the user needs to have at least one of. If the value field is empty all users can use the personalize list which is also the baseline behavior. If the user isn't allowed to personalize the list, the cogwheel icon isn't visible on the list view.

- **glide.ui.personalize_form:** This work similar as the property that handles personalization of a list view. Only differences are that this handles the form personalization and it can only be activated or deactivated for the whole instance. Here you can't e.g. define a list of roles that are allowed to do it.

- **glide.ui.permitted_tables:** In baseline configuration you can't do reports on system tables (starts with sys_). But if you someone need to do this, you can add the table to this property. Just do this with caution, since there is a reason why the system tables are not in the report list in the Baseline and you might end up with huge performance issues if you start to do reports on tables like sys_audit.

- **glide.ui.homepage.parallel:** This property turns on parallel homepage rendering. By using this, testing have shown that average performance on rendering a homepage has been around 20%- 50% faster.

- **glide.ui.homepage.parallelism:** This property sets how many threads the parallel homepage rendering is using.

- **glide.ts.global_search.parallelism:** Each search group you have for the global search uses a thread to render the search result. This means that if you for example have more than 4 (which is default value) it will search 4 groups first, then when a thread is free it will go on with the next group. Putting this higher will give better performance around search, but of course only if you have more search groups than your current value. So, if you have 4 search groups, you can keep the default value since raising it above the number of search groups doesn't give any performance raise since there already is enough threads to handle them.

- **glide.ts.max_wildcard_expansion:** This property holds the number of max search results that comes back from the global search. Default it has 500. Problem here is that if the search returns more than 500 values, it will return 0 and ask the user to refine its search query. Sadly, in the message it doesn't say that it found too many, it more looks like it didn't find any records at all.

- **glide.ui.session_timeout:** This holds the amount of minutes the user can be inactive before the apache webserver will throw out the user. It doesn't care about if you still active through your SSO (like e.g. ADFS), it will still force you to logon to ServiceNow again, which can make your current open windows to reload and so on. And that can lead to people losing information in fields they didn't save etc. Try to keep this value to be at least the same amount as your SSO if you have any.

- **glide.ui.reference.readonly.clickthrough:** Default this property is set to "false" and that means that if a reference field is "read only", there will not be a "i-icon" next to it where you can either hover to get more information or click on the get to the record itself. Remember setting this will affect all reference fields in the system. There is a specific field attribute you can use if you want to change the behavior on a specific field. Read more bout that in the field section.

- **glide.ui.impersonate_button.enable:** Use this property to turn enable and disable the functionality to see the impersonate choice in the banner menu. Default value is true, but setting it to disable will remove it for everyone. Remember that this will not remove the impersonate functionality. People with the role can still go to **https://<INSTANCE_NAME>.service-now.com/impersonate_dialog.do** and select a person to impersonate from there.

- **glide.ui.list_mechanic.roles:** This holds a list of roles that can use the personalize list functionality. With this a user can add/remove fields in the list view of records. Default it has no value which means that everyone can add/remove fields in list view.

- **glide.ui.update_on_iterate:** If you are on a list and clicks on a record you will get two arrows in the upper right where you can easy go to the next/previous record that was in the list. Default this property is set to **false** meaning that it won't automatically update the record you were on when you clicked on the arrows.

- **glide.entry.loggedin.page_ess:** specifies which portal/page an end user (user with no roles) is being redirected to after login. Might be overridden if the Service Portal properties is used. But this property also will be in affect if the user after login is trying to navigate away from the specific portal.

- **glide.rest.debug:** Use this to turn on/off the Rest debugging in system log. Default this is set to false, but changing it to true it will log the incoming rest with more information about the payload etc.

- **glide.ui.show_template_bar.<TABLENAME>:** This property is per table, and if you e.g. create "glide.ui.show_template_bar.incident" and set that to false, and the option **Toggle template bar** under **More options** isn't visible anymore for incident records.

- **glide.sla.calculate_on_display:** If set this to true, SLAs will be recalculated every time a record with SLA is being opened through a form. If it's set to false, the SLAs will be calculated according to the baseline SLA engine. There might be a performance decrease on form load when this is set to true, so make sure to test it before using it in production.

- **glide.ui.ref_ac.startswith:** When you start writing in a reference field, the autocomplete is starting to search. But default, it's searching with "contains" and that means that if you type in "k", it will return all results containing a k. That search can both return a big amount of search results and can also be a performance issue. Instead you can set this property to **true** and this it will change its search from a **contains** to **startswith**. Just remember that this property will affect all fields system wide.

- **glide.itil.assign.number.on.insert:** To stop numbers from being reserved but never being used since the record inserted, this property has been made so it only assigns a number when the record has been inserted. Don't let the name fool you, it applies to all tables with the numbering feature activated. It doesn't matter if the table is extended from the task table or not. It will affect all tables using the functionality.

- **glide.ui.activity_stream.style.comments:** If you want to have different colors in the activity stream (log) on the additional comment posts, you can set the color with this property.

  glide.ui.activity_stream.style.work_notes: Just like the previous property, if you want to have different colors in the activity stream (log) on the work notes posts, you can set the color with this property.

- **glide.invalid_query.returns_no_rows:** When you do a GlideRecord query and you have a invalid filter with e.g. addQuery, then the query will just ignore that condtion and return the records without that filter. If this value is set to true, it will return no rows if there is e.g. an invalid addQuery.or addEncodedQuery involved. But having this to true, it's a lot easier to find invalid queries since you will see nothing instead of perhaps just a few wrongful record.

- **glide.ui.textarea.character_counter:** if you have a string field with 255 characters or more it will appears as a multi-line text box. If you want, you can have a counter which shows how many characters they have left to type. If you want this, set this property to true.

- **glide.outbound_http.content.max_limit:** Sometimes you need to activate logging on e.g. outbound REST calls. Default value here is 100 which means that for example in your request body, you will only see the first 100 characters. And often, that isn't enough. So change this to a bit higher will give you all the data. Remember that changing the value will only affect new log entries, not the old ones.

Using gs.getProperty("property name")

When you later want to get the values of a property there is a function that you can you. It's very simple you your code could look something like this:

```
var getGrp = gs.getProperty("custom.incidentP1.group");
var gr = new GlideRecord("incident");
gr.addQuery("assignment_group", getGrp);//only wants
incidents that is assigned to this group
gr.addActiveQuery();//Just want to have active incidents
gr.query();

if (gr.next()){
//Do something fun.
}
```

Now, for this case it works without any trouble. But what you should be aware of is that gs.getProperty always returns a string. This means that even if you have a property that is set as a boolean (True/False) like this:

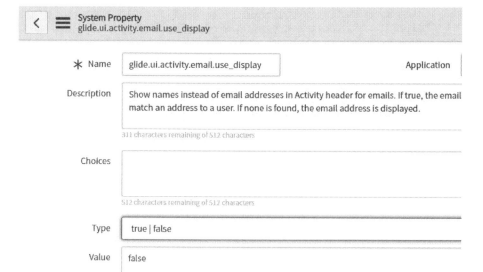

✳ Name	glide.ui.activity.email.use_display	Application

Description

Show names instead of email addresses in Activity header for emails. If true, the email match an address to a user. If none is found, the email address is displayed.

311 characters remaining of 512 characters

Choices

512 characters remaining of 512 characters

Type

true | false

Value

false

But the value field that holds the value is a string. The type field here is mainly for setting up a good User experience when using normal system properties modules:

Customization Properties for the User Interface

Property name: glide.ui.activity.email.use_display

Show names instead of email addresses in Activity header for emails. If true, the email address on a email address is displayed. ⑦

☐ Yes | No

Roles that can view email in the Activity formatter when including "Sent/Received Emails" ⑦

itil,sn_customerservice_agent

"Assigned To" image used in Activity formatter: ⑦

images/icons/user.gifx 🔍

Assignment group image used in Activity formatter: ⑦

images/icons/group.gifx 🔍

Where we can see the top property is a Boolean with a checkbox for you to set the value in. You can also hover over the question mark to see the property name. I showed you a good example where it still worked like a charm. Let's see an example where it doesn't work like you would expect.

I have created the following system property:

| ✳ Name | custom.test.boolean |

| Description | |

512 characters remaining of 512 characters

| Choices | |

512 characters remaining of 512 characters

| Type | true \| false |

| Value | true |

3996 characters remaining of 4000 characters

Now when I use gs.getProperty() to get this property and see if it's has a the Boolean value of true. I will not get what I was hoping for. Let me show you with this script:

```
var getProp = gs.getProperty('custom.test.boolean');
if (getProp == true) {
    gs.debug("Yey, a boolean variable");
}
else {
    gs.debug("Nope, not true");
}
```

And the result is:

[0:00:00.019] Script completed in scope global: script

Script execution history and recovery available here

```
*** Script: [DEBUG] Nope, not true
```

Since this is a string field, "==**true**" won't work. Here I would need to do "== '**true**'":

```
var getProp = gs.getProperty('custom.test.boolean');
if (getProp == 'true') {
    gs.debug("Yey, a boolean variable");
}
else {
    gs.debug("Nope, not true");
}
```

User preferences

Settings that is for the specific user is often saved in the user preference table. This is also the place where you can create default user preferences. Good to know is that even if you create a default value e.g. setting the form in **tabbed mode**; a user can always override the default with changing the setting and then it's their own setting that is used and not the default one. This can be stopped with a custom solution like for example having a before business rule aborting the save of a specific user preference. If doing this, remember to put up some kind of message for the user, otherwise they will have no clue it doesn't work for them.

How to create a default user preference

Sometimes you want to set a default value for a user preference and it isn't always easy to know what the preference is called etc. In this example I'm showing you how to set **tabbed forms** as default.

1. Easiest way to find out what the preference is named is to actually set the preference yourself and then go to the table and look for the last updated record. In this case I changed the value here on "Tabbed forms".

2. Now, let's go to the table and see.

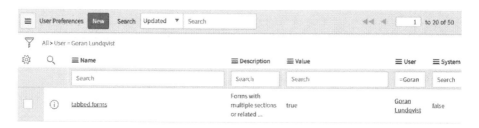

   After sorting on updated, you can see the preference being set for the user "Goran Lundqvist".

3. Now we can open up that record and use that for the default preference we wanted to have. This is how it looks like before we made the changes to make it a default value instead.

Now we only want to do two things. First is to check the system field and then to remove the value in the user field. After that it should look like this:

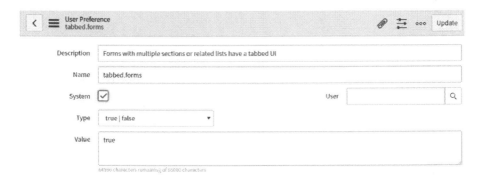

And that is it. Now, if there already are users that has a preference record, you can delete all those and then they will get the default one when they login the next time.

When it comes to update sets and user preferences, only the user preferences that are Global/default/system are saved within the update set. User specific preference (the ones that has a value in the user field) is not saved in the update set.

Useful preferences

As with system properties, after working with ServiceNow, some user preferences are more useful than other and can help you solve some requirements that you might has well.

- **list_edit_enable:** This property controls if the user will see the "insert row" at the bottom of a related list.

- **"Form personalization":** If a user personalizes a form on a table there is created a specific user preference for each view on that form. The name of preference is **personalize_<table name>_<view>**. For example personalize_incident_default or personalize_incident_mobile. The value has the fields that has been remove from the specific view on the form.

- **workspace.globalSearch.recentActions:** This is one of the new workspace preferences that are in use. In workspace there is a new global search that you use, and it remembers your previous search. Those searches are saved in this user preference. So if you want to clear the search history of a user, you can remove this specific user preference.

Handling licenses

This is always a question that comes along when someone is using ServiceNow. We all been there and asked or got the question "how does the license model work" and "Do we have the right licenses"? First of all, I always tell people who ask me this to contact their ServiceNow contact. Main reason for this is that the license model can look so different depending on the customer. It has been changing many times under the years and it mainly boils down to when the contract was signed and how did the licenses look like then.

Now for handling and administrating it, there is actually something you might be interested in and it comes along as a free application on your instance. It's called "subscription management". With this you can easily look how your licenses are being used and take the appropriate actions to make sure you are getting maximum value out from them.

Example of things you can do:

- Monitor how your subscriptions are being used over time and see how the usage is changing.

- Easily plan for how you should renew your subscription

- Use the application to allocate users to different subscriptions

Here is a good picture how it works which is from the docs.servicenow.com

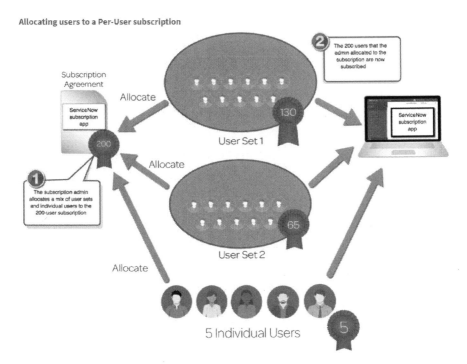

Allocating users to a Per-User subscription

© 2018 ServiceNow. All rights reserved.

In short terms you define what is needed to be defined as a user. For example if you have the **ITIL** role, you will count as a fulfiller of the ITSM subscription. What I'm missing is predefined conditions for the different subscriptions, but I guess the reason for it is that there are so many different versions of each application/suite that is hard to have predefined sets that will work. Might be a suggestion to ServiceNow to actually set these up for the customer when they are selling a new license to the customer.

And just remember that this application is only working on the production instance. This means that you can use this in your dev or test instance to play around with, but you need to do it in your production instance to have the correct license data in there as well. In your sub-production instances, there will be no license data around.

TABLES AND THEIR FELLOW FIELDS

In ServiceNow there are a lot of tables from the start. Sometimes they handle the requirements, but you will always come to a point where there might be need for a custom table. The requirements can even be as little as just having an m2m (Many 2 Many relationship) table to just make sure the relationships are in order for certain records. A good Baseline example of an m2m table is the **Group membership** (sys_user_grmember) table. This table holds the relationship between the users and the groups. And we all know a user can be in many groups and a group can have many members and that why it's called many-to-many relationship.

Baseline tables that are good to know

There are so many Baseline tables in ServiceNow and even more will be installed when you activate different plugins and applications. It also happens that when a new release comes, new tables for the existing applications are being installed as well. It's not easy to get information about these and they might just slip under your radar. Then you get a requirement and you start creating custom tables to achieve the same functionality as the new tables already is used for. One good example here is the table **Item Produced Records** (sc_item_produced_record). It holds the information about if a record has been created through a Record Producer. I'm trying to write down all these tables that I find and write them down to remember where I they are located. I have only kept the ones that actually don't have a module to them in the Application Navigator that I know of.

You can find more information about that table and other tables here:

- **sc_item_produced_record:** This table is holding the information about if a record is created through a Record Producer. It holds both which Record Producer record and which record that was created.

- **sys_user_grmember:** This is the table which holds the relationship between users and groups. In my early days, I didn't know this and finding it was a gold mine.

- **sys_user_has_role:** This table is similar to the group membership, but it instead holds the relationship between the users and roles.

- **sys_update_xml:** This tables holds all the changes that are done to configuration records. Both Baseline and custom records. If a record is logged in here, it will be skipped during an upgrade.

- **sc_item_option_mtom:** This table holds the relationship between the RITM and the variables and its answers. From this you can also dot-walk to the exact variable on the catalog item that is used.

- **sys_public:** This table is used to hold e.g. UI Pages that should reachable without a user having to be logged in.

- **m2m_kb_task:** This tables holds the relationship between attached articles and which task it has been attached to.

- **kb_use:** Keeps track on which articles which user has read.

- **ml_predictor_results:** Table that saves all the records that Agent Intelligence couldn't predict.

- **Sys_m2m:** This is the table where you have the many-to-many relationship tables. If you want to create your own many-to-many table, this is the place to do that.

Sometimes you end up looking at a record and you might not have a clue in what table that record exists in. Good example are related lists. Sometimes the label of the table will give you a hint, but others there is a simple way and that is in the URI. In this example we look at the user record, and at the related list call roles.

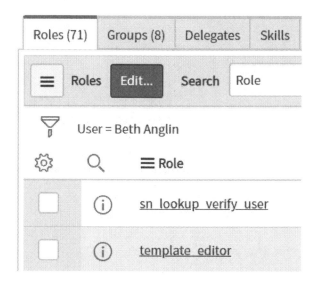

Here you might think that you see records from the roles table, but that isn't what you do. This related list is showing records from the table called "User Role" with the database name "sys_user_has_role". Now, one of the easiest ways to see the table is to click on one of the records in the list and look at the URI. Here you can see the database name:

service-now.com/sys_user_has_role.do?sys_id=2921c149db7ea340c

You will also see the real label of the table on the form. In this case it's "User Role":

Another way is actually right click to get the context menu and select **Configure->Table** to get to the table itself and see the name there like this:

Creating/Editing tables & fields

There are many tables within ServiceNow already and the more plugins/applications you will activate, the more there will be. But sometimes there will be a need to create your own tables to get the functionality you want and here are a few tips that I have ran into myself when I had to do it.

Sometimes I noticed that I suddenly don't have the option to **insert row** on an embedded list. After the last line there should be the **Insert a new row...** functionality, but it's gone and now it looks like this:

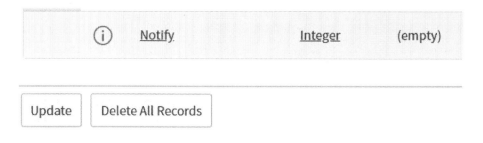

But it should look like this:

Now, I don't know the root cause if this, but I found out that it might actually be a user preference doing this. This also means that it might be gone for some people, but not for everyone. To get the functionality back you need to go to the User Preference table (sys_user_preference) and find the record with the name "list_edit_enable" and the correct user. Now this should be set to false and when you change it to true, you will get back the functionality. You might need to log out and back in again to see the change taking place. There should also be a default user preference which can also been set to **false**. This means that everyone that doesn't have their own specific user preference will use this.

Extending or not

When you create a table you can choose to either create a table from scratch or you can extend it from an already existing table. This is a decision that you need to take when you create the new table. Since after you have saved (submitted) for the first time, the choice to extend isn't available anymore and you need major customization to revert your decision. Now, not all tables is available to extend from and it all comes done to a field on the table record called **Extensible**. If this is checked, other tables can extend from this specific table.

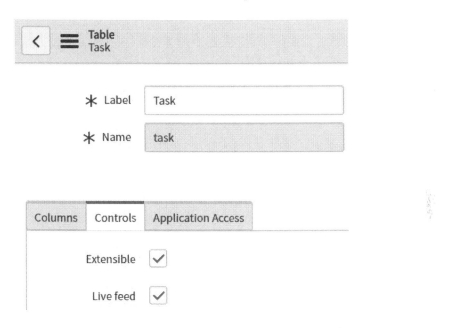

If you extend your new table, this will inherit all the fields that exist on the table you extended from. It might also inherit configurations like e.g. UI Policies and Client scripts depending on how they are configured. But those you can uncheck, so it doesn't run on "child" tables. This is done with the field **Inherited**.

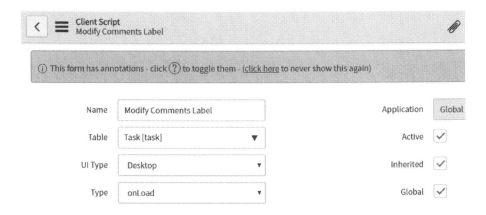

What is a bit tougher is the Business rules. They don't have a field like **inherited** like the client script has. But they still will run on all the different child tables of the table they are made of. To understand how to work around that is important to understand that even if I have an extended table, it still saves all the records in the table that your new table is extended from. E.g. is the task table. There are many tables extending from task. E.g. incident and change table is extended from task. This means that if you go into the incident table you will only se incident records and in change table you will only see change records. But if you go to task table, you will see all of them and many more. This is all controlled with a field called **Task type**.

Let's group by **Task type** and it will give a better overview:

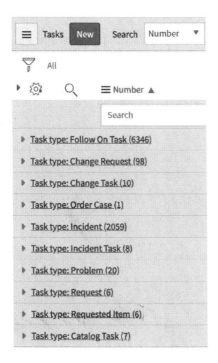

Here you can see that the different records have task type like Incident and Change Request. To come back to Business rules and if you want it to only run at task records, you need to specify that in the condition builder.

This can also be used if you want the same functionality in e.g. incident and Change, you can make the business rule on task and then as a condition set that type needs to be incident or change.

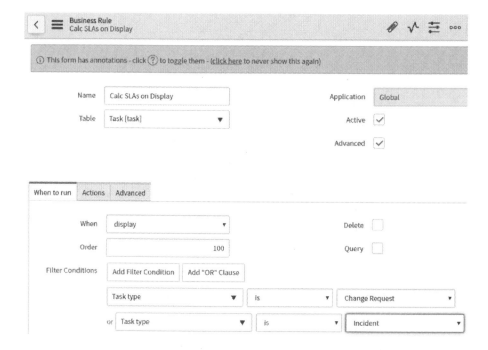

There is also another perspective on extending a table. You can basically extend from a table that is used by an application which you haven't a license for. By expanding from that table, you might violate the license agreements, so be careful if you not sure what the table is used for.

Extending from task or not

Before choosing to extend or not, some functionalities within ServiceNow only works on tables that are extended from task or the task table itself. To get these functionalities to work with other tables will require major customization and I wouldn't recommend doing that. Before you start creating a table, think about what the end game is for this table. You might not need workflows at the first release, but later perhaps?

Here are some examples of Baseline functionality that only works on the task table and the tables extended from it:

- **Assignment rules:** Functionality that is used to automatically assign records to groups or users depending on certain conditions.

- **Approvals:** Functionality that handles the approval records, both manual and automatically.

- **SLA:** To use the Baseline Service Level Agreement functionality the table that the SLA should be attached to need to be connected to the task table.

- **Workflow:** The workflow engine will only work on tables that are connected to the task table. Those are the only tables that are selectable in the table field on workflows.

- **Templated Snippets:** A way of handling response templates in a task which is an additional plugin which needs to be activated before used.

Good fields to have

When creating a new table, there is one or two fields that I always create on the table. Depending on what use the table has, that field is Active and Order. To make the administration of your table at a minimum, active helps me to sort out which records that is active. Just like the normal active field on the Baseline fields, I want this on my own tables as well. Keep in mind that the Baseline functionality **addActiceQuery()** that you might use when scripting doesn't work with your custom active fields. That functionality only works with the Baseline field. The Order field is nice to have when you have records that you often would like to be able to set in specific order. I don't use the Order field as much as the Active field.

Custom field

After a while as an administrator or developer you will end up in a situation where you need to create your own field. Now in ServiceNow there are multiple places where you can create those and so let go through the different places, the pros & cons for each place and of course, which place I myself like to create them.

But before I do that, I'm going to write a few lines of what you need to think of when creating a custom field, especially when it comes to tables that are extended from another table.

As going through earlier with tables, it also important to understand the consequences of where you create your custom field. In this example, we have gotten a requirement from our incident process owner that they want to have another field on the table called "secondary assigned to".

Now, first thing that you should ask yourself is of course "does there already exist a field like this or a field that I might be able to just relabel". It's important to ask this question because of several reasons.

- The process owner often doesn't have an overview of all the existing fields on the table. They only know about the ones that exist on the form and perhaps some other fields that they are using to create reports on.

- It's easy to just add another field. And then another, and another. That is one of ServiceNow's strengths as well as weaknesses. In some situations, it's too easy to just throw in another field before really understand if it's the right way.

- Some fields are not in use anymore and might be useful for you with only a relabelling of them. Before you do this, make sure to read up on the documentation about the field, so you don't start using a field which you perhaps will need in a year when you start using the functionality that the field was meant to be used with.

Now we have thought it through, and we need a new field. Next question that comes up is should we create this field on the incident table or the task table. This is also very important since when you have created it, it is where it is. There are ways of moving a field from the extended table (incident in this case) to the parent table (task), but it isn't something that I recommend doing. Better to think it through first time. So, what is the differences of having it on the incident table or the task table?

The biggest difference is that if you put it on the incident table, it will not show up on other tables that are extended from task. But if it's a field that many tables (that are extended from task) are going to use, then it might be a good option to put it there instead. If it's not, it better to keep it on the incident table to avoid the other tables getting bigger and cluttered with fields they aren't using.

Another thing to think about is reporting and lists. Depending on how your field is setup, it might be easy or hard to use that in reports. For the list, remember that if you for example is using the module "my work" which points at the task table, it will demand configuration by you as an admin to show that field, since a normal user can't dot-walk when they are personalizing their list view, but you as an admin can.

Now that you have decided to create a new field, there are a couple of different places that you can do this. So, let us walk through some of the most common ways.

Form layout

First place most people get to know to is through the form layout. This give you quite the easy way of creating a new field and you simple just need to decide on the label of the field and what type the field should be and press **Add**. You can't set much more options that this. But it's simple and quick.

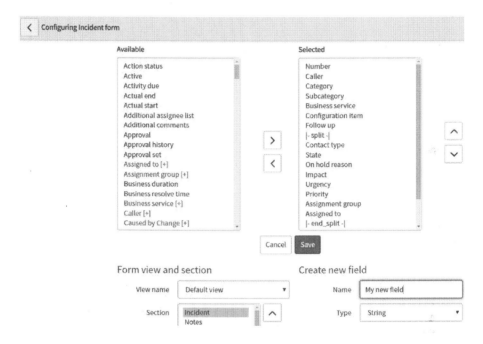

The negative part here is that you don't get to decide what the database name (column name) should be for this field. And you can't change this afterwards. So for the field I now created called "my new field" I got the database name of **u_my_new_field**.

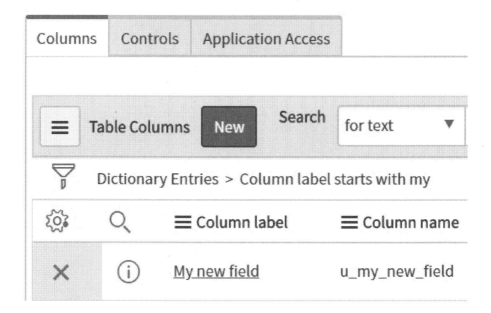

This wasn't that bad, but if I would have a longer label, then the database name could get really annoying, when you are going to write scripts on that field and use the database name. So it works like it should, but you will probably have angry developers on your tail when they are making scripts for this field. And I wouldn't say making very long database names is a good way to keep away from making scripts...

Form designer

Besides form layout, you also have the form designer. It's a bit more complicated with a few more clicks do create a field, but you can define the database name when you create the field, which is good.

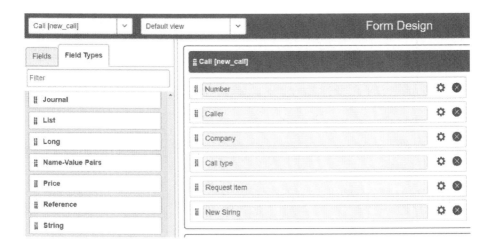

First you select the **Field types** tab. Then you click and drag over the field from the list on the left to the form on the right side. Now if you save, it will have the same database name as if you created it through the Form Layout. But you can change this as long as you don't press save. What you need to do is click on the **cogwheel** that is on the right side of the field.

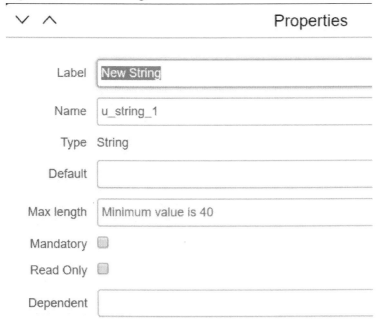

Here you can change the database name, which is the field called name here. You can also set more options as you can see here.

After you are happy, you can press Save on the form designer and close the tab. Now the field has been saved and are ready to use.

Embedded list on table record

Last place we are going to look at is on the table record itself. This is normally the way I go when I create fields since I feel that I'm in total control. When you open up the table record, you can see

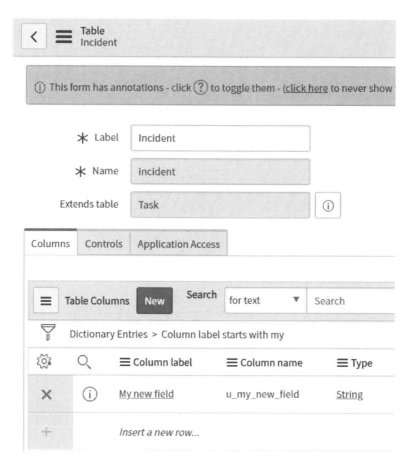

Now, you can either click on the new button or you can use the **Insert a new row...** functionality at the bottom. I normally go for this, but before I start to add new fields through the embedded list, I customize the list layout to also show the column name field. Now I also can decide what column name the field should have. If I leave it empty, it will create a default value that is the same as if I would have created the field through the form layout. But I can shorten down like this example if I want:

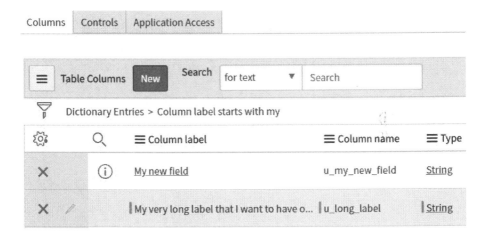

Now to get my new created field saved, I need to save the table record. If I don't save, the field will not be created.

You can also see a red X at some rows. This indicates that it's a custom field and I have the power to delete the field from the table. If I click on the X, the field will get crossed out like this and when I save the record, the field will be deleted from the table along with all the data that was stored in it.

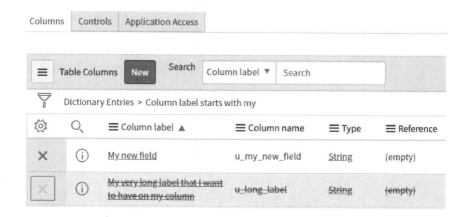

Remember that if click on a field that you just created and haven't saved yet then it will be removed directly.

Table & field naming

When it comes to give the table its database name you only get one shot. After you saved the record for the first time, you can't change it. You can change the label, but not the database name which you use in scripting later on. So in some cases it's better to just have a shorter label (since the name is created from the label) and then just change the label afterwards.

When it comes the label your table, make sure you always give your table a name in singular. This follows the standard of the Baseline tables where you have for example demand, change_request and incident. Then ServiceNow will add an "s" for the plural version. It sometimes also is smart enough to see that e.g. "showcase entry" will instead be "showcase entries" instead of "showcase entrys". But if it gets messed up, you can always change the plural form through the dictionary (sys_dictionary). Here you need to find the record for your table that has type "collection".

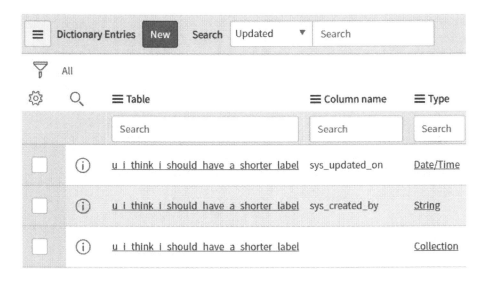

In here you can change both the singular- & plural label.

Same goes when creating custom fields. You will get your chance when you create the field to decide the field database name, then it's read-only. So remember the different ways from earlier, where you can either use the form designer or the embedded list on the table record to give access to decide the database name.

When you create a custom table or field, you might have noticed that the database name always starts with **u_**. This is ServiceNow's way of saying that this is a custom configuration/creation. And when another admin or developer comes along; it makes life a lot easier to understand which ones are Baseline fields and which are your own creation. Of course there are exceptions, and that is when you are building scoped applications. In there you actually don't need to have u_ on fields since it's your own applications. But it might be a good use case to have it, since if you e.g. extend a custom table from task, it might it harder to separate the custom fields from the Baseline fields.

And for the last advice, before you start creating fields, make sure you have a standard to follow when it comes to the field name. It might be recommended to follow some of the standards that exists within ServiceNow. E.g. is that all data lookup tables start with dl_, so when creating your own I recommend starting it with u_dl_ to make it simple to understand and also to easy filter tables to show only e.g. data lookup tables.

Table display value

When you look at the fields in a table you will see one column called **Display**. The field that has the value **true** is what the table display value is. With this means that it's that field that will be shown when other tables have fields that have a reference field to this table.

So only one field in the table can have the value "true" in the display field. The rest of the fields has the value "false". In earlier versions ServiceNow you could accidently have multiple fields having true as display value which lead to strange behaviors. Now there is a business rule that is automatically setting all other fields to false when you set a display field to true. But this can be an old setting that was configured before the Business rule can around and be worth looking into if you're having issues.

Then you can have tables where there isn't any field that has the value **true**. One example is the user table (sys_user).

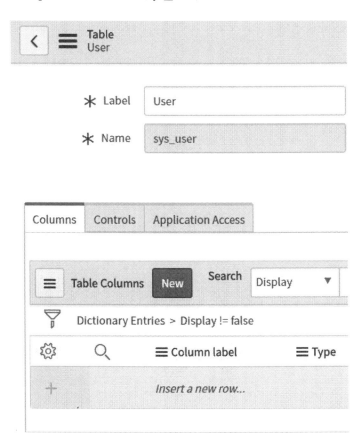

But still, you see a value on fields that reference to the user table. E.g. on incident table, we have a field called caller_id which happily shows the full name of the user you have selected. And the reason why, is that there is some logic in the backend how to handle tables with no display == true. And it does the check in the following order:

1. Check if there is any field on the table that has "true" in the display field.

2. Check if there is any field on the parent table that has "true" in the display field.

3. Check if there is a field with the name "u_name" or "name".

4. Use the created on field.

So as you can see in the user tables case, it comes down to number 3, then it finds the value it shall display in a reference field.

If you for example on the user table set the **display =true** on the email field like this:

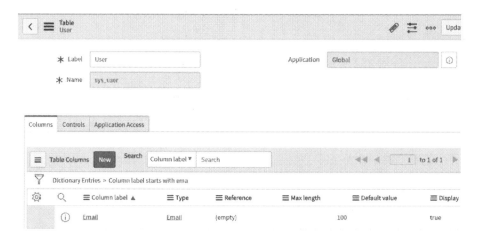

Then it will be the email that is the display value on the reference field that points to the user table. For example the Caller field:

		≡ Number	≡ Opened	≡ Short description	≡ Caller
☐	ⓘ	INC0012009	2018-12-25 15:28:10	Inc created through script	jerrod.bennett@example.com
☐	ⓘ	INC0012010	2018-12-25 15:28:51	Inc created through script	abel.tuter@example.com
☐	ⓘ	INC0011990	2018-12-20 14:01:02	test 2	abraham.lincoln@example.com
☐	ⓘ	INC0012001	2018-12-20 14:01:02	test 1	jacinto.gawron@example.com

Dictionary attributes

There are many different attributes that you can set in a field to make it act different. All attributes mention in this book and that you find in your instance should be documented and found on the https://docs.servicenow.com/. From there you either search for **Dictionary attributes** and filter on the release you are on. Then you should have a good search result where the top one should lead you to all the different attributes.

There is of course also a couple of ways to set this attribute and here I'm going to show two different ways of doing it and then you can decide if you want to use them or take another way of administration it. I can't see anything that is better than another, it's just what you personally feel. I would say it's about the same here as when you are going to administrate the form layout and choose between the form layout or the form designer. I normally go through the form and the fields there since it almost always a field that is on the form that you want to do changes on. From the form I right-click and choose the **Configure Dictionary** option.

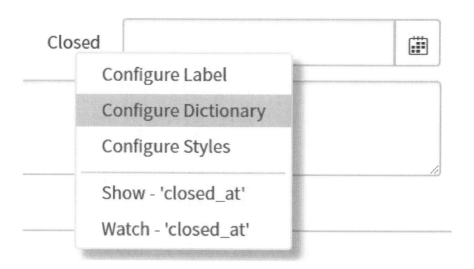

From here you can either use the field **Attributes** or the related list **Attributes**. If you don't see the **Attribute** field, click on **Advanced view** and it should show up Let's take a look at field first.

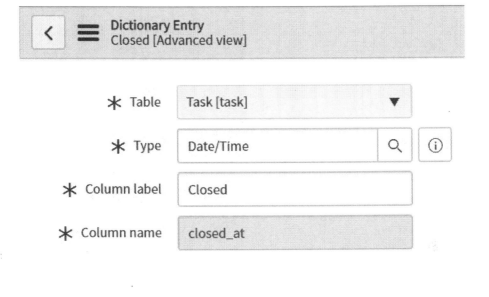

Here you can see that you have an attribute **sla_closure** which is assigned a value **incident**. And then it uses "," to separate each attribute. This is for me the quickest way of setting the attributes when you know what names they have and the values.

The other way you can administrate the attributes are through the related list. Here you can see it has the same attributes as show up in the field.

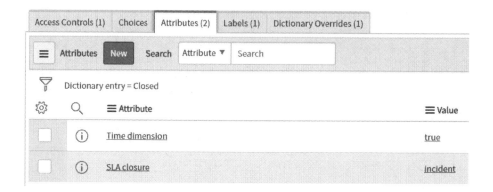

If you click on **New**, you get an easy choice to create a new attribute for this field. Here is the attribute field also a reference field for you to quick find the attribute you are looking for.

Now we have the new attribute in the related list.

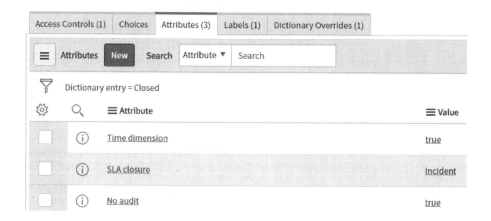

And actually the **Attribute** field is synced with this related list so you will see that it also has been updated.

Attributes: no_audit=true,sla_closure=incident,timeDimension=true

947 characters remaining of 1000 characters

And that goes on both directions. Meaning that if you remove an attribute from the field above and save. It will be removed in the related list as well

How to use the Baseline Active field in task

As you might have noticed, the active field on task and it's extended field will be set to true or false, depending on which state the task is in. In earlier years that was handled to through hard coded value and a lot of administration. Nowadays you can administrate this without any coding at all. The configuration has been moved into attributes on the table instead. We are going to look at how ServiceNow handle the functionality of closing a task, meaning it will set active to false. This will only be interesting if you decide to add another new **Close state** or perhaps want to change the which states is marked as Closed States. The foundation of this functionality is through a Business Rule called **mark closed**. Now, there are multiple Business Rules with that name and the one we are looking for are the on the **Task** table and looks like this:

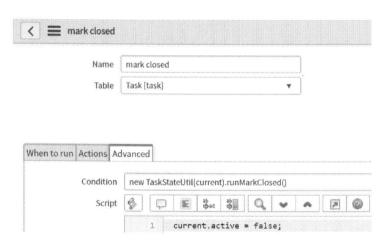

The interesting part here is what is written in the condition field:

```
new TaskStateUtil(current).runMarkClosed()
```

This calls the Script Include **TaskStateUtil** and runs the function **runMarkClosed()**. If that returns **true**, it will set the active field to false. Now, default there are three states that are marked as inactive states with the values 3,4 & 7.

- Closed complete (3)
- Closed Incomplete (4)
- Closed Skipped (7)

Now remember that it's the value (3,4,7) that is used in the script, so changes values on these states will give you very strange behaviors and not recommended. If there isn't any specific configuration on the extended tables, these are the three states ServiceNow will automatically change the active field to false. That means that if you e.g. only want to have one state on your custom table that should trigger this, then you can label the state to anything, as long as it has any of the three values (3,4,7). Then you don't need to configure anything more.

But sometimes you want to override these three values. How do you do that? That is simple done with an attribute on the state field. And this done through what is called a dictionary override. With this, you override what values it already has from the start. Let's play with the requirement that on incident table, we need to add a state called **Closed Workaround**. And by some reason this state needs to have the value 9.

All > Element = state > Table starts with incident > Language starts with en

Table	Element	Value ▼	Label
incident	=state	Search	Search
incident	state	9	Closed Workaround
incident	state	8	Canceled
incident	state	7	Closed
incident	state	6	Resolved
incident	state	3	On Hold
incident	state	2	In Progress
incident	state	1	New

Now, we go into the dictionary of the field and the easiest way is just to right-click on the field and choose **Configure Dictionary.**

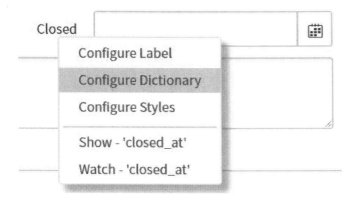

Now we are going to setup the attributes and it's easy to forget that you don't fill in the attribute field here.

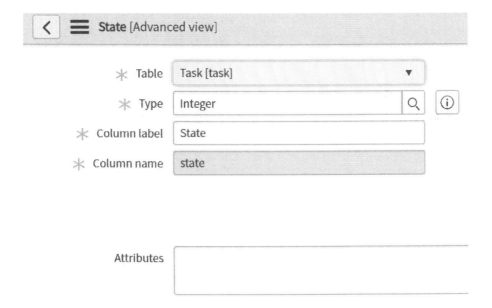

But as you can see this is the dictionary for the **Task** table. Configure the attribute here will affect the task table and every other extended table that doesn't have a

Dictionary Override on the attribute field. To make this for incident only, we need to go down to Related List **Dictionary Overrides**. Now Incident table already has a record for this field, but if there wouldn't be any, you can just click on **New** to create one.

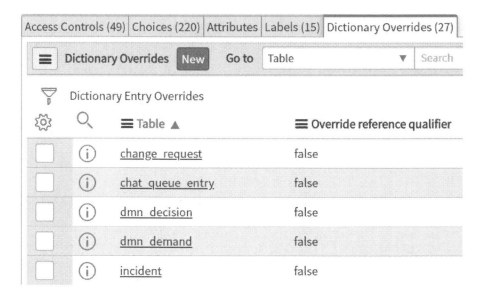

So now we just click on the incident record and can see that it already has an override for the attribute field.

What we are interested in here are two attributes. The first one is **close_states**. This defines which values that does count as an inactive state. Also worth looking at is the **default_close_state**. This attribute is used to override the **default close state** which is defined in the **TaskStateUtil**. In that Script Include there is a function called **getDefaultCloseState()** which is called to set the default value. But now we just want to add our new state to also count as an inactive state and we do that by just adding the 9 to the string.

```
close_states=7;8;9,default_work_state=2,default_close_stat
e=7
```

Remember that you uses **Semicolon** to separate the values.

This kind of functionality can definitely sneak in with a new release without making a big scene of it and easily missed if you don't look closely in all the changes. It can also be so that on an existing instance that is being upgraded you will need to activate a plugin, while on a new instance with the same release that plugin is activated in the Baseline configuration.

Useful attributes

Here are the attributes I have stumbled across and found useful over the years.

- **readonly_clickthrough:** This attribute can be used to make to either hide or show the "i-icon" on reference fields when the field itself is read only. If it's set to **true**, there will be an icon next to the field even if it's read only.

- **ref_decoration_disabled:** Continue down the path of reference fields, this attribute can be used to remove the "i-icon". If this attribute is set to **true**, it will never show up next to the reference field. Many people use DOM manipulation to get this functionality but it a lot better to use this attribute instead.

- **html_sanitize:** Sometimes the security of the HTML sanitizer is stopping you from putting in the things you want in an html-field. For example, it might block you from embed videos in your knowledge article. What you can do then is to give this attribute the value of **false** to let you embed the video. Now, this is tweaking the security, which means that you should use it with caution.

- **no_add_me:** This is useful on glide list fields like watch list or work notes list. If the value is set to **true**, the icon for "add me" disappears.

- **json_view:** You might have noticed that some fields containing XML has a little XML icon at the label which will give you a popup windows with all the xml in a nice format. This attribute will make your life easier on JSON data. You set this attribute to **true** on a string field that contains a JSON

65

string. It will give you an icon next to the label which will give you a popup with the JSON data in a nice format. Just like the XML button.

- **max_unit:** I was and still am sometime very confused with duration fields. First time this happened was on SLA records where it said that the duration was e.g. 1 day, 2 hours, 10 min. In my world I interpreted it as it was 1 "SLA day", 2 hours and 10 min. I didn't realize it the duration was 26 business hours and 10 min which really was more like 3 business days in real life. Now setting the value of this attribute to **hours** will remove the day and you will instead get see "26 hours, 10min" which I like a lot better. I also think this would give a better overview in reports as well that also are affected of this attribute. You can of course here have other values (**days/hours/minutes/seconds**).

- **no_filter:** if you have a glide field and don't want to have the filter in the slushbucket you can set this attribute to **true**. By doing that, the filter in the slushbucket will vanish.

- **ref_ac_columns:** This attribute has multiple purposes. It can be used to define which fields that is visible in the dropdown when you start typing in a reference field with autocompleter activated. But it can also be used to limit which fields that is actually being searched through when you are filling in the reference field. Then it must be used together with the attribute ref_ac_columns_search=true.

- **no_attachments:** If you have a table where you don't want the user to be able to attach files to the records this is the attribute you need. Go to **Configure -> Dictionary** and find the **Collection** record of your table. Add this attribute to that record.

Default value

Default value is a nice and simple way to define the value a field should have if nothing else is put into that field. There are a couple of ways you can set the default value.

First out is just the value like 1 or hardware. Remember when configuring the default value, it's just the value you should put in and not the display value or label. A good example is the state field that is on the task table. Where the default value is just 1, but in for example incident table that is converted into the state "New" which has the value 1.

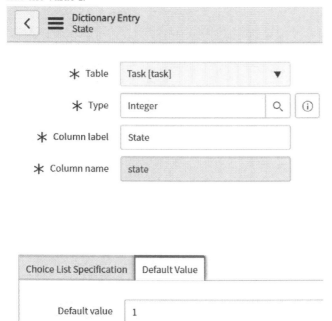

The second way you can do with default value is to use JavaScript to define the value and give it more a dynamic value than a static one. For example, if you want a date-field to always default when a record is created to be 7 days ahead of the current day you can do like this.

Last out is the dynamic default which you might have seen being a nice checkbox on the pictures above. If you can't see it, it is because it doesn't appear in the **default view** and you need to switch over to **advanced view**.

By checking the **Use dynamic default**, it will remove the default value field and show a reference field for the dynamic field options. This is a way to make dynamic fields that you can reuse. So instead of writing the same JavaScript code as the example above, you can do that in a dynamic filter and then reuse the filter in multiple places. When you later want to change something in that code, you only need to do it in one place and then it will affect all the places it's in use. This instead of editing all those fields manually. Here is an Baseline example that sets the first day of 2020.

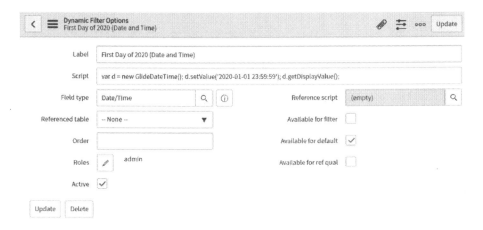

As you can see, the checkbox for **Available for default** is checked meaning this can be used in the default value fields. We will talk more about dynamic filter option later in this book and where else you can use them.

Calculated Value

If you go to the dictionary of a field, you will have a tab called **calculated value**. To see it you might need to click on the related link **advanced view** first to see it. There you will have a checkbox and when you check it, a nice field with some default code appears and in here you can write code to do a calculation of what the value should be:

Before we dig deeper in here, just to explain the difference between calculated value and default value. Default value is the value that is set if there isn't any other value in the field when the record is saved for the first time. Calculated value will automatically recalculate when the record is queried.

Now, this sounds cool and handy to use. But there a quite a downside here and I wouldn't recommend using this at all since this can be a real performance killer.

So why is that? The biggest reason is that the code you write here will run every time the row is read. If you have big complex code or just a simple dot-walk (meaning doing a round trip to server to get data) it will run. So, if you have a list of 100 rows, that code will run 100 times before the list is shown. It also runs even before the Business rules run, then under some circumstances, it might even run again after the before business rules run. And I guess the picture I'm painting here doesn't look pretty.

Instead of using the calculated value field, I would recommend trying to investigate having a before Business Rule to handle the code and update the field.

The reason I started to use this field once was that created a report on a duration field and didn't like the fact that the duration wasn't always up to date. But using this calculated value, I always got the "real time" value of the durations of all the fields I saw in the report. But in the end, I removed it again since it wasn't worth all the other issues that started to appear with performance.

Database views

Database views main purpose is to make the life of creating reports a lot easier and comfortable. When you create a report, you can only select one table that you want to base your report on. Pretty common you want to create a report which is based on multiple tables. A good example is a report on SLAs. All the information of the different SLA records is stored in the table called **task_sla**. When you then want to create a report on incident records and their SLAs you need to choose either the SLA- or the incident table. And the trouble starts on what fields you can use and so on. To help you out here there is something called Database Views. With this you will create a "virtual" table which is multiple tables joined together.

Here is a picture how the database view "incident_sla" looks like. One incident (in this case **INC0000060**) has multiple SLAs connected to it and therefor generates multiple rows in the list. One row for each SLA.

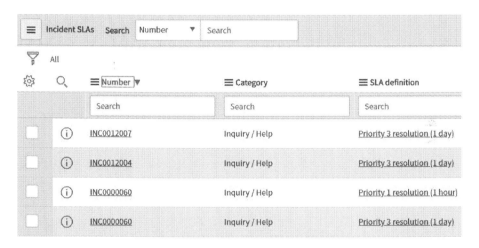

As you can see, here we can have columns from both the incident & SLA-table and that is the good part about using database views.

Now, depending how the database view is setup not all records are being visible in the list. E.g. in the incident_sla view, you will only see incident that has a connected SLA. If an incident doesn't have any SLAs connect, it will not show up in the list. In this case it's of course a good thing, but sometimes you want to see all the records. To do this you need to use something called **left join**. This field in on the table form for the matching tables which we will go deeper into how to configure a bit further down. But for this field you probably need to configure the form to make it visible like this:

In the case of incident_sla view, and if we want to see all the task_sla records even if we don't find a matching incident, we need to check the "left join" on the view table record for incident. After doing this, you will have a list view of incident_sla that looks like this:

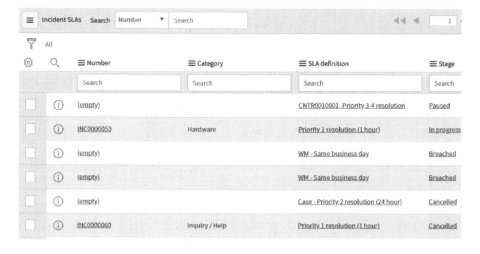

Where you can see "empty" in the number field if the task_sla record is pointing to another table than incident.

Here is another example that might come in handy. Sometimes I been asked to take out a list of all users that doesn't have a role or isn't a member of a group. In this example I'm showing how to see all users that isn't member of a group. For that we are making a database view connect two tables together. It's the User-(sys_user) and Group Members (sys_user_grmember) table. Then we take advantage of the left join functionality to say that I want to see the user records, even if they aren't in any user field on a group member record. Remember that you don't use a **dot** when you are writing the where clause. Instead you use **_**. In the case below we write **grpmem_user = sysuser_sys_id** instead of **grpmem.user = sysuser.sys_id** which would probably feel most correct in the ServiceNow world.

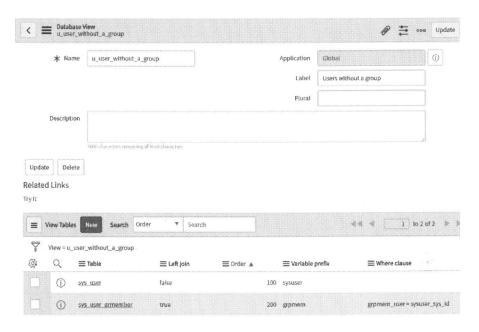

Now we get a list that we need to make sure it at least has the name column since that is how we see which user it is. And after that we just need to filter out the records that is empty in the group field (since then there isn't a group connected to that user).

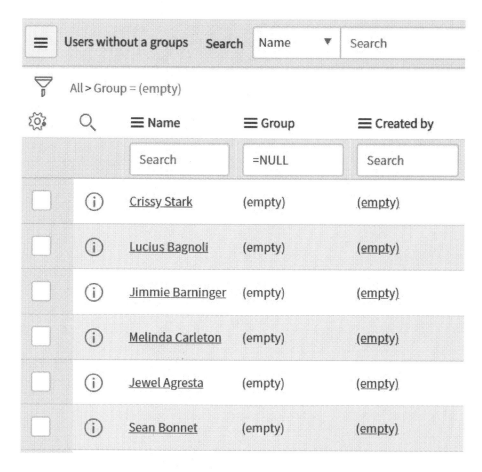

The database view honors the ACLs of the tables that is being joined and there isn't any need to create specific ACLs for the database view. It's still an option if you for any reason want to do it, but otherwise if the user can read the tables separately, they can also see the database view. If you are having a database view with multiple tables (3+) you can get strange behaviors though if the user doesn't have access to all the tables within the database view. Make sure that the user that is using the database view do have access to the correct tables.

When we are talking about access and what is visible, it's good to know that query business rules aren't making any changes to the queries when the database view is checking. For example, there is a Baseline query Business Rule for the user table which basically adds to **active==true** if the users isn't an admin. This means that normal users can't see inactive users when they look. It really looks like they see all users since the filter says **all**. This means that in a database view that is using the user table, normal users are seeing inactive users as well.

Difference between using a Document ID field and a reference field

From time to time the question pops up on the community. When should I use the Document ID field type and when should I use the Reference field type? There is some difference between them, so let's look a bit closer on them.

Reference field: With a reference field you are limited to a single table, you can't have a reference field that is pointing to multiple tables. For example, is the assigned to field on task referencing to the user (sys_user) table. Dot-walking functionality is of course working on a reference field and is widely used within many areas in ServiceNow.

Document ID field: A field with this field type can be used to point on a record in any table in the ServiceNow instance. But the field can't work on its own. Since it's only storing the sys_id, it also needs to know the table where the sys_id is from. When it has those two fields, you need to set so the Document ID field is dependent on the table field. A good example of this is the Approvals (sysapproval_approver) table. There you have a Table field called Source Table and a Document ID field called Approving (document_id). Sadly, on this field type you lose the ability to Dot-walk.

I would say that besides you need two field to get a Document ID field to work, the main difference is the ability to Dot-walk otherwise you can achieve most of the same functionality with both. It all boils down to what you want to use the fields for. If you need to be able to point to records from more than one table, then you can't use reference fields, but you need to sacrifice the functionality of Dot-walking.

Audit of a table & fields

One thing that you might find useful is to configure Audit on specific tables and fields. You have seen the work of audit on some tables like incident and so on where you can in either the activity field or through the context menu go to **History->Calender** or **History->List**. From here you can see all changes that has been made, when and by who.

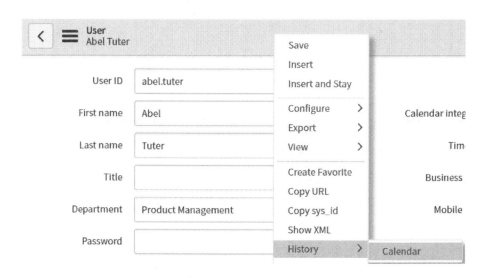

If you go to a table that doesn't have audit turned on, you will only see the Calendar option and when choosing it, you get a message that the record isn't being audited.

Now, you can easy turn on audit on a table, and you do that by going to the dictionary record of the table, let's take User (sys_user) as an example, since you actually may want to have audit on it which isn't by default.

All information about the record and what has changes is stored in the Audit (sys_audit) table. Now, as you might guess, this is a table is taking a huge load since it's keeping track of millions of changes in different records. But it's not working alone, to keep the performance up, it is working together with the History Set (sys_history_set) table. This also means that you shouldn't give into makes customizations on these tables unless you really know what you are doing.

Since Audit is holding so many records, stay away of queries or reports on this table. It's a big performance threat and I've seen records taking a couple of minutes to load because of a display business rule query a table with a couple of millions of records. And that amount might be nothing compared what the audit table handles.

If you decide to keep track of changes on a table, you can make the life of audit table a bit easier by setting the attribute **no_audit** on a field which means that it should not audit the changes on that field.

IMPORT & EXPORT

DATA

Now, there is a lot of different ways of handling import & export of data and how to do it always depend on a lot of different parameters. Here are a few examples of questions to ask yourself that hopefully will help you in your decision on how to setup the import

- Is it a onetime deal or something that should happen on regular basics?

- Is it a pull or push integration? Meaning does ServiceNow pull the data from another source or does another system push the data into ServiceNow. There are many ways of importing data, and depending if it's a push or pull integration, the method may vary. Everything from an excel sheet to Scripted REST API. The same goes for exporting data.

- How complex is the data? Do we need to clean/manipulate the data before it's imported into the tables in ServiceNow?

- Make sure the data that you are importing into ServiceNow is as cleaned up as possible. It's often a lot easier to clean up and fix the data before you have imported it than afterwards.

In this chapter we are going through the most common ways of importing and exporting data from and to ServiceNow. Hopefully some tips and tricks how to handle different scenarios and give you some pointers on how to start and where.

Transform maps

One way to go is using the import set process. Summary is that you will import the data in into a **import table** then you will use 1 or more transform maps to put this data into the "real" table(s). The import set acts like a staging table which holds the data temporary and then with transform maps you map the data into different tables and fields. You can also manipulate data before and/or after it has been inserted into the correct table.

If your imported data need to go into multiple tables, you need to create one transform map per table. You can even have multiple maps pointing on the same table, even if it doesn't seem to make any sense doing it. A good example with multiple transform maps is if you are importing in Configuration Items and their relationships into the Configuration Management DataBase in ServiceNow. Let's say you have an excel sheet with servers and which you want to import and then automatically create a relationship between them. For this you might have an excel sheet that looks like this:

	A	B	C	D
	E1 ▾ : ✕ ✓ ƒx	User:		
1	Server:	Serial Number:	Router:	Manufacturer:
2	A001	abc1343	Net001	Cisco
3	A002	sad3563	Net002	Cisco
4	A003	gjk3467	Net003	Cisco
5				

Column A & B belongs to the server CI record and column C & D is for the router CI record. It's not unusual that you will get data that will belong to multiple records on the same row. Another example would be having both users and groups the same row as this:

9		
10	**User:**	**Group:**
11	Wade Wilson	CAB approvers
12	Clark Kent	Service Desk
13	Bruce Wayne	Hardware

But back to our servers and routers. when you import those, you also want to set the relationship that the specific router is "Depended on::Used by" the specific server. For this you will need three different transform maps since we are importing data into three different tables and both the servers and routers has multiple columns that we want to save on their records. In the example we want the servers to go into the table Windows Servers (cmdb_ci_win_server), routers should go into the table IP routers (cmdb_ci_ip_router) and the relationship is setup in the table CI Relationship (cmdb_rel_ci). Now, we only need to load the data into the import set table once, then we can just run all the different transform maps at the same time, just need to remember to run them in the correct order. Since we don't want to try to create a relationship if not both the servers and routers are already there.

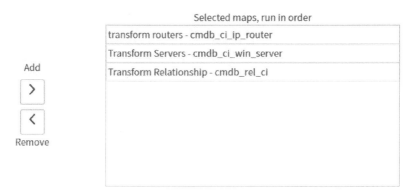

Sometimes when you import you can do a short cut to make it simpler. In this case it won't work, since the reference fields in the CI Relationship table for the server and router points to the table Configuration Item (cmdb_ci) and that isn't the place we want them to be. But if we look at the example about users and group. We could apply that with one transform map. The reason for it that we only want to fill in one field on the user table and one on the group table as well. For this we are using an option called Choice Action. With this we can decide what to do if we are trying to put in a value that doesn't exist in the target table of the reference field.

The field will be visible when the target field is a reference field or a choice field. Here you can setup 3 different choices to what to do when the row has a value that doesn't exist in the target reference field.

- **Create:** This choice will create a new record in the target table of the reference field.

- **Ignore:** This choice will ignore this specific value and continue to create the row (record).

- **Reject:** This choice will reject the whole record(row) that had the value. It will reject the row and continue with the next row in the import set table.

Copy empty fields

One thing that has trouble me in the beginning was how it default handles empty fields. In my case this was the import of users from an AD and where I used the Baseline functionality of the LDAP import.

If we look at the Baseline transform map for LDAP User Import it looks like this:

Most common is that you take this configuration and just trim it a bit to match your own which normally is a pretty simple deal. In Baseline, this will also set the manager of the user as well, which is a nice feature to use.

Anyway, the problem here is the **Copy empty field**. As you can see, it isn't checked by default, and this means that if there is field in the AD that is empty, it won't "copy" that over to ServiceNow. And in real life it shows work like if there is a value in a field in ServiceNow, but in AD there isn't anymore; then it won't update the field in ServiceNow to become empty. A more concrete example would be if a user has a business phone in AD and that is imported to ServiceNow. Then the user will by some reason erase that number in the AD. If the field "Copy empty fields" isn't checked when the next import is run, the import will just ignore that field and keep the number as it was in ServiceNow.

So, make sure to think it through if you want this field to be checked or not before you start importing data.

Run business rules

Another thing that might generate issues is the "Run business rules" and here we are talking about performance issues in peculiar. Baseline this is checked and in most cases it's any problem. But if you are perhaps doing a major import with millions of records, it can be a big issue. Especially if you are importing into a table that is being indexed. The experience I had from this was that the indexing job became so big, that the first indexing job wasn't finished before the next one was queued up. And the evil spiral just kept winding up. Pretty quick there was a delay on the index for all fields for a few days. This affects everything and one example if someone created an incident, that incident number wouldn't be indexed asap as it normally does and search for it returned zero results. It didn't show up until that index has been executed after a few days.

Easy import

One way of doing a quick easy import is through a functionality that ServiceNow calls "Easy import". This functionality will remove a few steps for you and can in some circumstances be a good enough solution for the import process. What it does it is that it handles all the transform maps and gives you a nice template in excel that you can use to either update existing records or import new records.

To take advantage of this you just go to the table you want to import data into. Right-click on one of the column labels and choose "import".

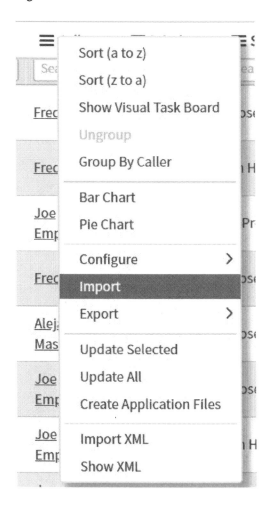

Now you get to another window where there are a few settings to choose from. Most important is if you are going to import new records or you want to update existing. If you are going to update existing records, remember that the excel file that is being created, it will have the records that is in the list. Make sure to filter the list correctly until you choose to create an excel template by clicking on the "Create Excel Template" button here.

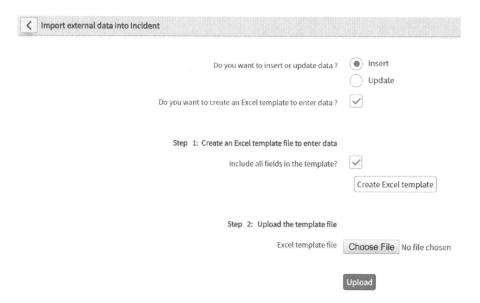

Then you can either stay on this page if you just are going to do a quick few changes or you can navigate away and do other things in ServiceNow while the excel file is getting ready to be imported again.

When the file is ready for import, you just do the same steps that you did to create the file, but in this case, you don't press the "Create Excel Template" button. Now you do the Step 2 part where you upload the file and click on "Upload".

Use xml export & import

Another way to import and export data that is quite common when we talk about moving smaller amount of data between instances. For example moving a couple of group records that was created in the developer instance and needs to be moved to the test- & production-instance. This is simple done by going to the table that holds the data and filter the list to only show the records you want to move. When this is done, you just right-click on one of the column labels and choose export and then XML.

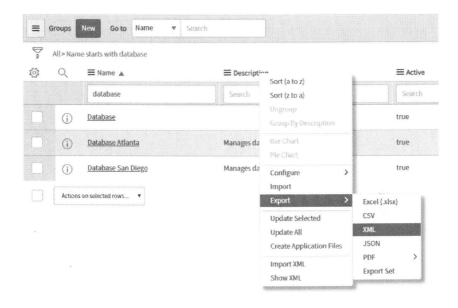

That will give you a popup window that when it's done gives you the option to download and save the xml-file.

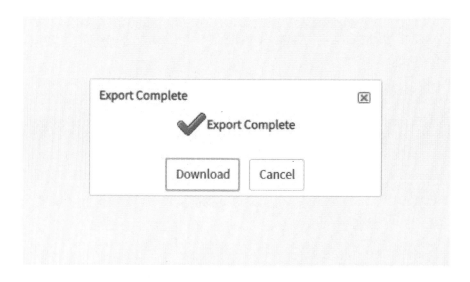

After you have downloaded the file you can login to the destination instance and actually go to any list. That is correct, it doesn't have to be the same table list as when you exported the records. The reason for this is that in the xml-file, it says to which table you are importing the records to. The only thing you need to do is right-click again on a label, but this time choose the Import XML and select you file. Then it is loaded and ready to be used.

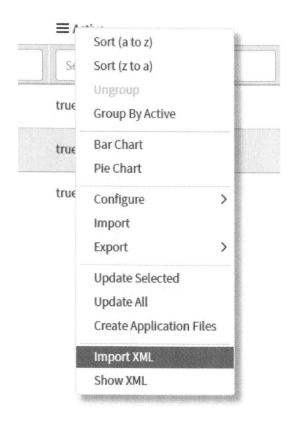

LDAP configuration

LDAP configuration is something that most customers setup and for the better part, there is an excellent baseline configuration that you can look and reuse a lot of it to make it work.

One issue that I have ran into is the password for the user account that is used to read from to the LDAP.

I couldn't log in with the user even if worked like a charm when I tested it outside of ServiceNow. The issue ended up showing that if the password has some special characters, it didn't work. In my case my password contained the hashtag (#) character and directly when I changed to the password to something "easier" it worked spot on.

Besides this, there is two other baseline functionalities that is good to know. first is the Manager and source setup. If you look at the transform map **LDAP User Import** which is used for the user import. After opening it, you can see in the script field; there is code for both setting up the manager of the user through the manager field on the user record and the source field.

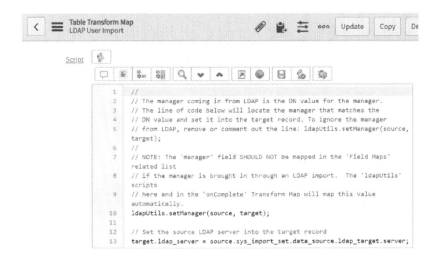

To get this to work 100%, you also need to copy over the Transform Script that is onComplete and looks like this:

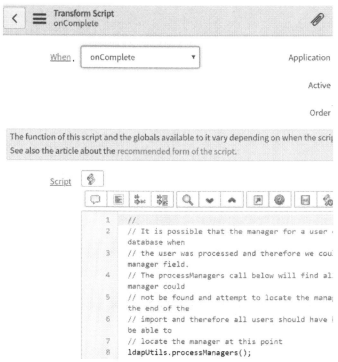

This is to use if the user was imported and their managers records wasn't already created. Then it will run this to make sure all users have the correct manager.

The second part that might be useful to reuse from the baseline functionality is the way to handle active/inactive users. You will find this in the Transform Script that is onBefore:

Script

```
1    //Deactivate LDAP-disabled users during transform based on
     'userAccountControl' attribute.
2    //This transform script is inactive by default
3    //
4    //NOTE: User records must be visible based on the OU filter
     disabled
5
6    //Convert the userAccountControl attribute to a hex value
7    var ctrl = parseInt(source.u_useraccountcontrol, 10);
8    ctrl = ctrl.toString(16);
9
10   //The relevant digit is the final one
11   //A final hex digit value of '2' in 'ctrl' means disabled
12   if (ctrl.substr(-1) == "2") {
13       target.active = false;
14       target.locked_out = true;
15       if (action == 'insert')
16           ignore = true;
17   } else {
18       //Optional: Reactivate and unlock the user account
19       //target.active = true;
20       //target.locked_out = ctrl.substr(-2, 1) == "1";
21   }
```

This might require adjustments depending on how your company handles users though. I have been with customers that move the inactive users to a separate OU which isn't in the integration and then this baseline script won't work.

CLONING

First let's just talk about how the cloning works in a light version:

- You request the cloning with the System clone->Request Clone. Remember that the data you are cloning are default from last night backup. If you just changed something, you must set the clone date for tomorrow instead if you want your last changes to be cloned, unless you want to clone from a live production instance which isn't recommended.

- Now it looks at the "Preserve data" table and see what data on the target it should save. The data is stored somewhere else(magically) and will be restored after the clone.

- Copies over everything to the target. If the table is in the "exclude tables" it only copies over an empty table.

- Then it copies over the "preserved data" that was stored before the copy.

- Runs the post-clone clean-up scripts.

How to save data on the target

System Clone->Preserve Data. Here you specify which data you want to save on the target. You can take a whole table or you can set conditions like everywhere else in ServiceNow to just get a specific records from a table.

Now, preserve data does one thing, and that is make sure that the data on the target exists after the clone. It **doesn't** stop data from the source to be copied over. If you only fill in the "Preserve Data". It will have data from both the source and the target. Example is the table "update sources" which holds information from which instance you get your updates from. If you put that table in "Preserve Data" it will keep your target source, but it will also copy over the sources "update sources". In real life this will probably look like if   you clone production to test, you suddenly have the productions update sources, which is the test instance.

What you need to do is to put the table in the "exclude tables" as well. Then it will first only copy over an empty table, then copy back the preserved data from the target.

The "Exclude audit and log data" checkbox

There is also one checkbox I want to talk about and it's "Exclude audit and log data". This checkbox is checked as default and will stop a huge chuck of data to be copied over. And most of the time it's not needed. But it means for example that workflows aren't copied over, so if you after the clone go investigate change requests that were copied over, they won't have a workflow connected to them. And that also means for example that the UI Action "Show workflow" isn't visible. It also excludes the audit data which means that the activity log for those records are messed up with time stamps and so.   The fix for this is of course to uncheck the field, but unless you have good reason to do this and copy over an extra-large amount of data, I recommend not to do it. Since you should still be testing with new records/tickets anyway to see that it all works as intended.

Amount of data copied from task table

More and more instances starting to become quite big and have a lot of records in the task table. And sometimes you want to clone with some of this data to have a test data, but not all of it. From the London release there is an option for this when you request your clone.

Now you can at least choose if you want to clone with all the data from the task table (including incident, change etc.) or only records that was created in the **last 90 days**.

Custom Applications

Also remember that if you are developing custom applications, those also needs to be saved/preserved in some way. When you clone from production to e.g. your developer instance it will copy over the application version that exists on production. It will become editable, but it will not have the draft version you might have been working on in development. The best way to handle this is through the source control. For example, let's say that on your source instance, you have version 3.0. but on development you are building 4.0. If you clone you will have 3.0. on development as well. But after you cloned, you can connect it to your source control and then commit the latest changes and you will be back on version 4.0. on your development instance.

SERVICE CATALOG

Service Catalog is a well-used application in ServiceNow, and it feels like the more the customers use ServiceNow, the more functionality in the catalog is being explored and used as well. For each new release, there are new functionalities within this application and I feel that a lot of power is being used to make the user experience in the Service Portal as good as possible.

Request Vs Requested Item

One question that comes up sooner or later when it comes to the process with the Service Catalog is how does it with the process of creating Requests and Requested Item? We all probably know that there is one Request that can have multiple Requested Items connected to it. Sometimes you will come to the stage where you want to customize the process and what data it will contain. To do this it's important that you know how to process works.

Let's say that you want to copy something from the requested item to the request record. First thought and without knowing anything else I would probably create a business rule on the Requested Item to just by script query and get the request record and update it with the requirements I got. This would work fine, if the request is already been created. But what if the request still hasn't been created. If we turn on debug and look what happens when we press the *Order Now* button in the catalog. And I'm not going to show all the rows in the debug, since that would make this a very thick book.

```
01:08:52.982: Execute before insert business rules on sc_req_item:RITM0010007 before engines (order <1000)
01:08:52.982: Global ==> 'Task Active State Management' on sc_req_item:RITM0010007
01:08:52.983: Global <== 'Task Active State Management' on sc_req_item:RITM0010007
```

As you can see, one of the first things that is running is the before Business rules on the Requested Item. And these are running before the Business rules of the Request. This means that the Requested Items are created before the Request which doesn't really make any sense, but that is how it works. So, my Before Business rule on a Requested Item to update the Request would fail, since the Request record hasn't been created yet. Good to know here is that the workflow for the Requested Item isn't been triggered yet, but we talk more about that later.

```
01:08:53.81: Finished executing after insert business rules on sc_req_item:RITM0010007 after engines (order >=1000)
01:08:53.102: Execute before insert business rules on sc_request:REQ0010007 before engines (order <1000)
01:08:53.102: Global === Skipping 'Message Associated Record to Request' on sc_request:REQ0010007; condition not satisfied: Filter Condition: parentISNOTEMPTY^EQ
01:08:53.102: Global ==> 'Task Active State Management' on sc_request:REQ0010007
```

Now you can see that the after Business Rules for the Requested Item has been ran and now the before Business Rules for the Request is starting to run. The major different behaviour here comparing to the Requested Items is that the Workflow for the Request (if there is any) will be created and started. If there isn't anything stopped the Request workflow to be completed like an approval or wait condition the workflow for the Requested Item will start. When the Request workflow has ended which means the approval field on the Request has changed, the following Business Rule runs and sets the fields approval and stage on the Requested Item. This business handles all three scenarios of what type (Workflow, Flow or Execution Plan) of process record is connected to it.

```
01:08:53.413: Finished executing after insert business rules on sc_request:REQ0010007 before engines (or <1000)
01:08:53.424: Execute after insert business rules on sc_request:REQ0010007 after engines (order >=1000)
01:08:53.424: Global ==> 'Cascade Request Approval to Request Item' on sc_request:REQ0010007
```

When that business rules have set the values on the Requested Item (which also means that the Requested Item record is being updated) the business rule below triggers and starts the workflow or flow for the Requested Items that are connected to the Request.

```
01:08:53.439: Global === Skipping 'Start FlowDesigner Flow' on sc_req_item:RITM0010007; condition not satisfied: Condition: !current.cat_item.flow_designer_flow.nil() && current.stage=='request_approved' && current.flow_context.nil()
01:08:53.439: Global ==> 'Start Workflow' on sc_req_item:RITM0010007
```

With this being said, the short story of the Request Vs Requested Item would be.
- The Requested Item records are being created before the Request record is being created.

- The Request starts its workflow directly after the order has been made in the Service Catalog, while the Requested Items doesn't start until the Request part is done.

Variables

Variables are a vital part of the Service Catalog and it's hard to have a catalog without them. What is needed to understand is that depending on where in ServiceNow you are looking at an item, the variables might look and behave differently. There is a good description on the documentation site for each variable, if they work at all in the Service Portal or if there is any limitations.

The variables I have noticed that are behaving differently is these:

- **Containers:** One of the biggest changes in behaviour is the containers. If you select the *Display Title* option, you will in the normal UI have a expand/collapse icon which will function on the whole container and its variables. It will also have a question mark icon to show the help and instructions that you have filled in on the variable. But on the Service Portal the expand/collapse functionality is gone, and the help and instruction are always visible. On the normal UI it looks like this:

And on the Service Portal it looks like this:

Container start

My helpt text on contain

my instructions

- **Email:** There is a baseline validation of the value to see that it is an email-address. This only works in the normal UI. The validation isn't running if you are coming through the Service Portal.

- **HTML:** When it comes to the HTML-editor, it almost works the same way on both places. The difference is that a few different format buttons in the editor depending on where you are. One example is that in the normal UI you won't have the paragraph option and in the Service Portal you won't have the Font Family and Font Sizes choices.

- **IP-address:** This variable type has the same problem as the Email variable. In the normal UI there is a validation check on the value that the user writes, but it doesn't work through the Service Portal.

- **List Collector:** The List collector is one of the variable types that looks totally different depending on where you look at the variable. If you go through the normal UI, it will appear as a so called slushbucket while in the Service Portal you will have the look as a dropdown field. On the Slushbucket you also will have the option to set a filter manually, which isn't available on the Service Portal.

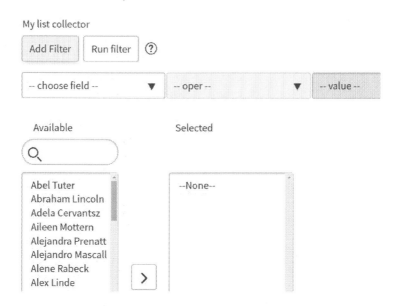

While on the Service Portal it looks like this:

My list collector

My list collector

- **Macro & Macro with label:** These are very special variable types. They can be used on both the normal UI and the Service Portal, but depending on which place, it needs different configurations. If it should be working with the normal UI, it needs to be using the Macro or summary macro field. If it is supposed to be working in the Service Portal you need to use this with the Widget field. Reason for this is that the Macro & Summary Macro fields requires macros with Jelly code. That doesn't work on the Service Portal. For that you need to build the same functionality within a Service Portal Widget instead and link to it in the Widget field.

Read/Write/Create roles on variables

There has been added new functionality to handle the certain access to a variable. Now you don't need to make a Catalog UI Policy to make a variable read only. Sometimes you want a field to be populated with specific data depending on a value from another field that the user fills in. And this variable should be read only since it's only to show the end user the value. This is one of the requirements you can use these fields for instead of making a UI policy to handle it. The fields I'm talking about is on a specific section called *Permission*.

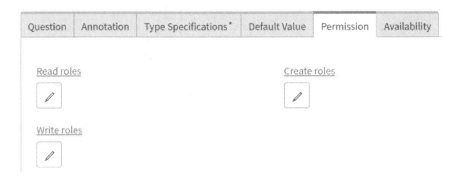

If the field is empty, that means that all users has the functionality that the field is for. To explain more what the fields functionality is:

- **Read roles:** This field is used to specify who can see the variable. Both on the Catalog Item/Record Producer and on the record created after submitting.

- **Write roles:** This field is used to specify who can change the value in the variable editor AFTER the record has been created through either a Catalog Item or a Record Producer. If the user doesn't have the roles specified in this field, then the field will be read only AFTER submitting.

- **Create roles:** This field is used to specify who can create a value for the variable itself BEFORE the Catalog Item or Record Producer has been submitted. If the user doesn't have the roles specified in this field, then the field will be read only BEFORE submitting.

Example Text

One functionality that came within the recent release is the ability to have a placeholder text in a field. It has the same functionality as the placeholder attribute that exists within the HTML language. This is a good way of giving the user a hit of what is expected in the field. Not all variables have this functionality, but if they have, you will find a field called *Example Text* that you can fill in the placeholder text you want to have.

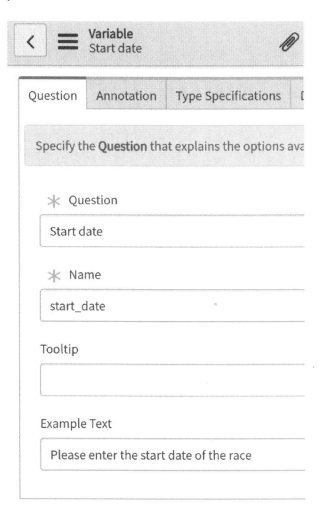

And when you come to the item in the Service Catalog it looks like this:

Start date

Please enter the start date of the race

Variable type "Yes / No"

Now, on the normal tables there isn't a "Yes / No" field type that you can use. Closest would be either a Boolean field (true/false) or a choice list field. There are some negative parts of those two since Boolean always has a value and therefor can't be set as mandatory and a choice list, well, then you need to maintain choices and remember to include a **none** choice, then build some nice functionality to not accept that choice.

Now for the type "Yes / No" all this already is fixed. The two choices are there and there is also a nice checkbox you can check to include the "none" choice and then easily make it mandatory, so the user needs to choose either Yes or No.

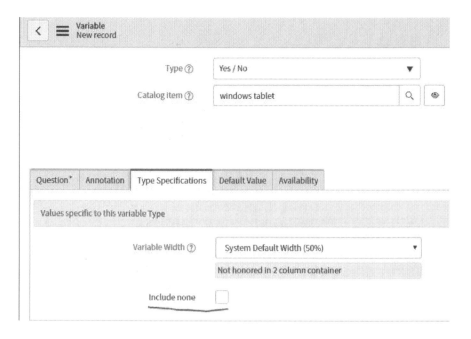

Multi-row variable set

In earlier releases there has always been requirements of an easy way of handling multiple inputs. What I mean by this is that for example you want to have a variable where you might have a couple of fields and then you can add extra rows with different data. In this example let's say you want to put different users into different groups. Earlier you would need to go into some major customization to get a good look on it, but with multi-row variable set you will have an easy way forward.

What we are looking for it this:

Gorans Multi cool set

Actions	Who to curse?	Which Curse?	Extra text
✎ ✕	Abraham Lincoln	Angry Chicken	Real tasty
✎ ✕	Beth Anglin	Bloated feet	Like Big foot
✎ ✕	Alejandra Prenatt	Angry Chicken	

Here we have one column which is reference variables to the user table, one Multiple Choice column and one string column. None of these are mandatory and you can see that Alejandra doesn't have anything in the **Extra text** field. Remember this for later practice with scripting. With the Add button we can easily add another row with data and use the pencil- and x-icon to edit or remove a row.

Now to get from zero to the look I have above is just a few simple steps and let's see what you need to do to achieve the same thing.

First just go to the catalog item or record producer you want to add it to. Then click on new button that is on the related list for variable set. Here you will now get a choice on which type of variable set you want to create, and in this case, you choose of course the **Multi-Row Variable Set**.

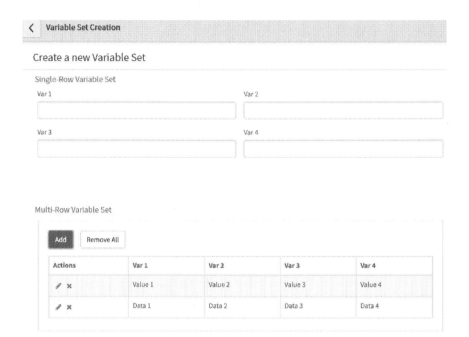

Now it looks like a normal Variable Set, but the major difference is that all variables that is created here is becoming their own column in the row that the end user will see.

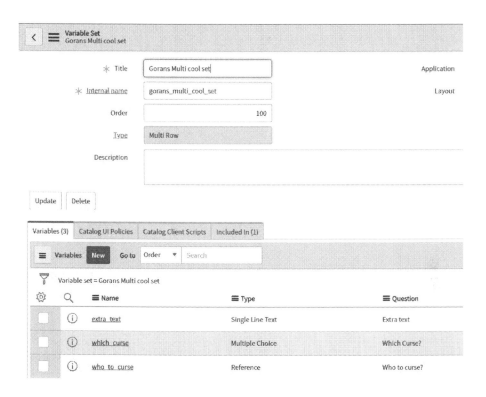

And when the item has been ordered, this is how it will show up on the requested item (RITM).

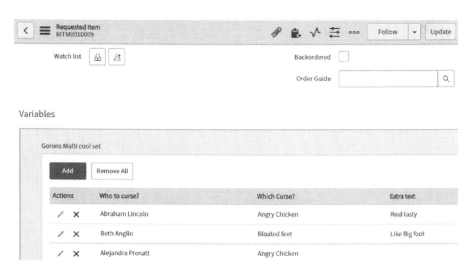

There are also a few things you can do if you choose to use scripting to some magic with the variable set. Before we leave this subject, let's look at what you can do with scripting and Multi-Row Variable Set.

Let's first look at what we get if we look at the existing record above and the variable set.

Running the following script with data from the Requested item created from the example above:

```
var returnedSet;
var ritmID = '3c0381a0db0627002288dc50cf9619d6';//sys_id
of the RITM being created
var getRITM= new GlideRecord('sc_req_item');
if (getRITM.get(ritmID)) {
    returnedSet = getRITM.variables.gorans_multi_cool_set;
}
gs.debug(returnedSet);
```

Gives us this:

[0:00:00.221] Script completed in scope global: script

Script execution history and recovery available here

```
*** Script: [DEBUG] [ {
  "who_to_curse" : "a8f98bb0eb32010045e1a5115206fe3a",
  "which_curse" : "1",
  "extra_text" : "Real tasty"
}, {
  "who_to_curse" : "46d44a23a9fe19810012d100cca80666",
  "which_curse" : "3",
  "extra_text" : "Like Big foot"
}, {
  "who_to_curse" : "22826bf03710200044e0bfc8bcbe5dec",
  "which_curse" : "1"
} ]
```

What we can see here is that we get back an array with each row as a JSON object. As you can see, we get the field name and not the label. And we also get the value of the data in it and not the display value of the data. Also good to take into account is that on the last row, we didn't have any data in the **Extra text** field and how this shows up isn't through an attribute (extra_text) with empty value. Instead that JSON doesn't have the attribute at all. This is **very** important to understand if you are going to do scripting where you might loop through different attributes.

What you can also do if you want is to add new rows through scripting. And there you can use at least 2 different ways to put data into the new row.

```
var returnedSet;
var ritmID = '3c0381a0db0627002288dc50cf9619d6';//sys_id
of the RITM being created
var getRITM= new GlideRecord('sc_req_item');
if (getRITM.get(ritmID)) {
    returnedSet = getRITM.variables.gorans_multi_cool_set;
}

var newRow = returnedSet.addRow();
newRow.setCellValue('who_to_curse',
'5137153cc611227c000bbd1bd8cd2005');//sys_id of a user
newRow.which_curse = 1;

gs.debug(returnedSet);
GetRITM.update();
```

As you can see in the code above, you can use both the **.setCellValue()** function to set the values or just using to normal way with using the "=". To save the new row(s) for the RITM you just need to update that record which you can see I do with the last line **getRITM.update()**;

Public catalog item or Record Producers

Sometimes you might get the requirements to have a Catalog Item or Record Producer open for user to use without being logged in. If you have temped to do this with the baseline widgets you probably have run into trouble and can't get it to work. It's easy to make both Service Portal Page and widget public, but one thing that doesn't show up for the user that isn't logged in is the variables. And without them, it's pretty hard to make anything for the user. Depending on the requirements, you might instead solve this through a custom widget with a form. A good example is on the consumer portal (csp) where there are a form to register new consumers.

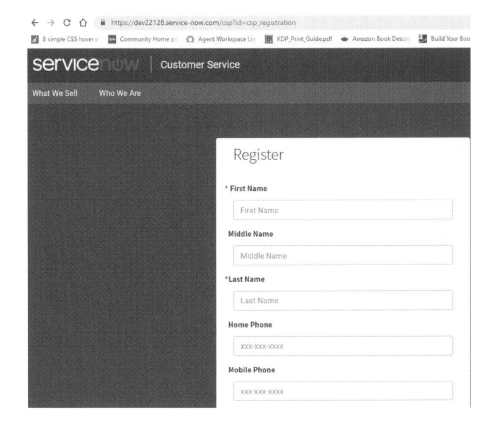

If you don't have this portal, you need to activate the application Customer Service here:

Q customer service

14 results for "customer service"

Customer Service
Customer Service Management

The Customer Service Management application enables you to provide service and support for your external customers using several ...

ID: com.sn_customerservice | Paid | by ServiceNow

And the portals that belong to that application which you can find here

Q *mer service portal

3 results for "*mer service portal"

ID: com.snc.appointment_booking | Free | by ServiceNow

Consumer Service Portal

Customer Service Management

Enables the Consumer Service Portal, a web-based portal based on the Service Portal application that your company can use to provide ...

ID: com.glide.service-portal.consumer-portal | Free | by ServiceNow

Customer Service Portal

Customer Service Management

SERVER–SIDE CODING IN GENERAL

This chapter contains general things I found that is applicable within the Server-side of ServiceNow. It involves coding in general and can be used in specific places like Business rules, UI Actions etc. I have noticed that this is one area in ServiceNow that does changes over the releases and what worked or was best practice for a couple of releases ago might not be it anymore.

First thing I would like to mention a very simple way of keeping your code nicely formatted and indented. This works in most places like the script editor and even when you are coding in widgets for the Service Portal, even in the html field on the widget. But it won't work in e.g. **Scripts – Backgrounds**. And I have no clue what the short key for this is on a Mac, so you guys need to figure it out yourself. But on Windows, you first hit **Ctrl + a** to mark everything and then you just hit **Shift + Tab**. And voilà, it's got that nice format that you are looking for. This is an example of a base line widget where I just messed up the html code since the baseline code is already nice formatted.

Goran annoucements ▼ Show ☑ HTML Template ☐ (

HTML Template

```
 1 ▾  <div ng-class="['panel', 'panel-{{::c.options.color}}', 'b',
 2 ▾  <div class="panel-heading">
 3 ▾  <h2 class="h4 panel-title" aria-label="{{::c.options.title}}
 4     </div>
 5 ▾  <ul ng-if="::(c.totalAnnouncements > 0)" class="list-group"
 6 ▾  <li ng-class="['list-group-item', {'can-expand': a.canExpand
 7 ▾  <style ng-if="::c.options.use_display_style" ng-init="::(ds
 8 ▾   li.{{::cssId}} {
 9     background-color: {{::ds.backgroundColor}};
10 ▾  text-align: {{::ds.alignment.toLowerCase()}};
11     }
12
13 ▾  li.{{::cssId}},
14 ▾  li.{{::cssId}} .details div.title div,
15 ▾  li.{{::cssId}} .details div.title a,
16 ▾  li.{{::cssId}} .details a.info-link {
17 ▾  color: {{::ds.foregroundColor}} !important;
18     }
19
20 ▾  li.{{::cssId}} .details p {
21     font-weight: 100;
22     }
23
24 ▾  li.{{::cssId}}:hover .details div.title a,
25 ▾  li.{{::cssId}} .details a.info-link {
26     text-decoration: underline;
27     }
```

Now I just mark all with **Ctrl+a** and then hit **Shift+Tab** and it change and looks like this.

HTML Template

```
1  <div ng-class="['panel', 'panel-{{::c.options.color}}', 'b', 'spw-
2    <div class="panel-heading">
3      <h2 class="h4 panel-title" aria-label="{{::c.options.title}}">
4    </div>
5    <ul ng-if="::(c.totalAnnouncements > 0)" class="list-group" styl
6      <li ng-class="['list-group-item', {'can-expand': a.canExpand,
7        <style ng-if="::c.options.use_display_style" ng-init="::(ds
8        li.{{::cssId}} {
9          background-color: {{::ds.backgroundColor}};
10         text-align: {{::ds.alignment.toLowerCase()}};
11       }
12
13       li.{{::cssId}},
14       li.{{::cssId}} .details div.title div,
15       li.{{::cssId}} .details div.title a,
16       li.{{::cssId}} .details a.info-link {
17         color: {{::ds.foregroundColor}} !important;
18       }
19
20       li.{{::cssId}} .details p {
21         font-weight: 100;
22       }
23
24       li.{{::cssId}}:hover .details div.title a,
25       li.{{::cssId}} .details a.info-link {
26         text-decoration: underline;
27       }
```

Creating new GlideRecords

Now there are at least two ways of creating new records through scripting. I'm going to go through the two most common ways and see what is different between them.

When you are writing code and want to create a new record you can use two functions. Here is two examples of the use of **initialize()** and **newRecord()**. Earlier I have been thought that the main difference between those two functions was that **initialize()** didn't use default values and **newRecord()** would take in account of the default value if there wasn't anything else specified in the code. But nowadays that isn't any difference **AFTER** the record has been inserted. So, what is the difference between the two functions? It's pretty much all in what you get before you save the record into the instance. To give a better explaining on what is happening, lets run some code to test and show what the result is.

```
var record = new GlideRecord("incident");
gs.debug("\n****** Without any function ******");
gs.debug("record Active is: " + record.active);
gs.debug("record Number is: " + record.number);
gs.debug("record Opened at: " + record.opened_at);
gs.debug("record Sys ID is: " + record.sys_id);

var recordInit = new GlideRecord("incident");
recordInit.initialize();
gs.debug("\n****** with Initialize() function ******");
gs.debug("recordInit Active is: " + recordInit.active);
gs.debug("recordInit Number is: " + recordInit.number);
gs.debug("recordInit Opened at: " + recordInit.opened_at);
gs.debug("recordInit Sys ID is: " + recordInit.sys_id);

var recordNew = new GlideRecord("incident");
recordNew.newRecord();
gs.debug("\n****** with newRecord() function ******");
gs.debug("recordNew Active is: " + recordNew.active);
gs.debug("recordNew Number is: " + recordNew.number);
gs.debug("recordNew Opened at: " + recordNew.opened_at);
gs.debug("recordNew Sys ID is: " + recordNew.sys_id);
```

What I basically do is create three objects and look at what some values a few fields have in the object before saving it. One object without using any of the functions and then one object each per function. The result from the script about looks like this.

Script execution history and recovery available here

```
*** Script: [DEBUG]
****** Without any function ******
*** Script: [DEBUG] record Active is: undefined
*** Script: [DEBUG] record Number is: undefined
*** Script: [DEBUG] record Opened at: undefined
*** Script: [DEBUG] record Sys ID is: undefined
*** Script: [DEBUG]
****** with Initialize() function ******
*** Script: [DEBUG] recordInit Active is: false
*** Script: [DEBUG] recordInit Number is:
*** Script: [DEBUG] recordInit Opened at:
*** Script: [DEBUG] recordInit Sys ID is:
*** Script: [DEBUG]
****** with newRecord() function ******
*** Script: [DEBUG] recordNew Active is: true
*** Script: [DEBUG] recordNew Number is: INC0010008
*** Script: [DEBUG] recordNew Opened at: 2018-11-25 00:32:42
*** Script: [DEBUG] recordNew Sys ID is: 7b2ad5e8db0627002288dc50cf9619dc
```

If we look at the results we can see that if we don't use any of the functions, the fields get the value **Undefined** which you can in short say they are not empty, they are still waiting to be defined.

Next test in the script is by using the **initialize()**. Here you can see it doesn't care about the default value in active field and it's set to false. The rest of the fields are **empty** and doesn't care about default values there either. But if I don't set any values on these fields, they will have the default values after being **Inserted**.

Last up is the **newRecord()**. Now you see that it got default values in all the fields even before the record is being **Inserted**. Worth noticing here is that you also have a value in the number field. This means that it will reserve a number. Looking at our script result above, you can see that it has the number **INC0010008**. This leads to that if I go to create new incident, it will have the number **INC0010009**, since the code has already used up the previous number even if it hasn't been saved. To stop this from happening, there is a system property to only use numbers when a record has been inserted. To read more about it, take a look at the system properties section in this book.

So depending on what kind of result you want, use either **initialize()** or **newRecord()**. Looking at the baseline scripts in ServiceNow, the majority is using initialize() and not newRecord().

Counting records

It might seems an easy way to for example count the numbers of records with a a GlideRecord query and then use the **getRowCount()** to get how many records you have. Your code would look something like this:

```
    var gr = new GlideRecord('incident');
gr.addActiveQuery();
gr.query();

gs.debug(gr.getRowCount());
```

But there is a better way to do this and also a better performance way when it comes to doing queries like SUM, COUNT etc. To do get the same result as the example above the code would look like this:

```
    var countInc = new GlideAggregate('incident');
countInc.addActiveQuery();
countInc.addAggregate('COUNT');
countInc.query();
countInc.next();

gs.debug(countInc.getAggregate('COUNT'));
```

This is just one thing you can do with **GlideAggregrate()** so don't forget that it exists. When it comes to mathematic requirements, take a look if you can do it with this API first before doing it with something else.

But then again, there is always an exception to the rule. Let's say for example that you are only interesting to see if there it at least one record in your query. You don't care how many or which, just if there is at least one. A requirement can be like that you doesn't allow a task to close if there it at least one sub-task still active. Then the **GlideRecord** that is fastest. Take a look at this script:

```
    var checkUser = new GlideRecord("sys_user");

    checkUser.addActiveQuery();
    checkUser.setLimit(1);
    checkUser.query();

    if(checkUser.hasNext()){
     gs.debug("Found one!");
    }
```

Now, why is this fast you may ask. And the magic lays in **checkUser.setLimit(1)**. It limit the result to query the database and when it finds 1 match it stops going through the rest of the records that exist. This means that if the second record of 100.000 is a match, it doesn't go through the rest of the records which is 99.998. The function **setLimit()** is a nice performance

Nested queries, the road to performance issues

Sometimes the easiest code, can end up being a real performance killer. Mostly people only talk about client scripts and how making server calls can be a performance issue. But the same thing can easily happen on the Server Side. One of those things that can create these issues is nested queries.

Now what is a nested query? It boils down to that you make one query and while you are looking through the results, you make another query each time you go to the next record in the loop. Here is an example:

```
var  getUsers = new GlideRecord('sys_user');
getUsers.addActiveQuery();
getUsers.query();
while (getUsers.next()) {
var getIncidents = new GlideRecord('incident');
getIncidents.addQuery('caller_id',
getUsers.getUniqueValue());
//the rest of the code.
}
```

Looking at the above code. First it will do one server call to get all the user records that matches the query. Then when it loops through all those records it will make another call to get the incidents. Now, if there were for example 100 users, it will be a total of 101 (one for the user call and 100 for looping through all the users and query for incidents) server calls. And you can see where this is going when it could be a lot more than 100 users.

Now the same result can be achieved with only 2 server calls. And the solution is using an array to save the users from the first query and then just do another call getting all the incidents belonging to someone of the users that is within the array. Here is an example of a remake of the example above:

```
var getAllUsers = [];
var getUsers = new GlideRecord('sys_user');
```

```
getUsers.addActiveQuery();
getUsers.query();
while (getUsers.next()) {
getAllUsers.push(getUsers.getUniqueValue());
}
//So now we got all the users sys_id from the first query
var getIncidents = new GlideRecord('incident');
getIncidents.addQuery('caller_id','IN',getAllUsers);//This
line says that caller_id should be any of the sys_ids in the
array.
//The rest of your code.
```

As you now see, we only had 2 server calls which will give you a lot better performance than the first example with 101 Server calls.

Another thing that also counts as a Server Call and is easy to forget is dot-walking. If you in the first example has something like this in the while loop:

```
var getUsers = new GlideRecord('sys_user');
getUsers.addActiveQuery();
getUsers.query();
while (getUsers.next()) {
var city = getUsers.location.getDisplayValue('city');
//the rest of the code.}
```

This is would also end up in 101 server calls. This since the location value is a sys_id on the user record and we need the display value. With the **.getDisplayValue('city')** in the backend it does another server call to check what the displayValue is for the record with the sys_id that was stored in the field on the user table.

Dot-walking is an easy way to get what you want. But keep in mind what it does in the backend as well.

Dot-walking in query

As dot-walking to get a value can be a performance issue, it can also be if you put it in the query itself. It's very easy to be carried away and do it since it so simple to write as code but remember that it might be a ticking bomb if doing it. Let's take a look an example. We want to get a list of all users that has actually logged in the last 5 minutes and is a member of at least 1 group. For that we could run this code and it would work but doesn't really have the best performance.

```
var minutesAgo = 5;
```

```
var members = [];

var getLoggedInUsers = new
GlideRecord('sys_user_grmember');
    getLoggedInUsers.addQuery('user.last_login_time','>=',gs.m
inutesAgo(minutesAgo));
    getLoggedInUsers.addQuery('user.active', true);
    getLoggedInUsers.query();


while (getLoggedInUsers.next()) {

var gpMember = gp.user.toString();

if (members.toString().indexOf(gpMember) == -1) {
members.push(gpMember);
}
}
```

In this case, it means that for each record in the **sys_user_grmember** it needs to do 3 server calls. 1 to get the record, 1 to get the **user.last_login_time** value and 1 to get the **user.active** value. If the **sys_user_grmember** table has 1000 records, it requires 3000 server calls to actually get through the 1000 records. This query will run a bit quicker, since there will be cashed queries unless not all 1000 records have unique users, which they probably don't. This can now be lowered from 3000 server calls to 2. And we use the same architecture as in the earlier examples which is based on store the first query results in an array.

```
var minutesAgo = 5;
var members = [];

var userRec = new GlideRecord('sys_user');
    userRec.addQuery('last_login_time','>=',gs.minutesAgo(minu
tesAgo));
    userRec.addQuery('active', true);
    userRec.query();

while (userRec.next()){
members.push(userRec.getUniqueValue())
}

var gp = new GlideRecord('sys_user_grmember');
    gp.addQuery('user','IN' , members);
    gp.query();

var resultUsers = [];
```

```
while (gp.next()){
  if (resultUsers.toString().indexOf(gp.getValue('user'))==-
1){
    resultUsers.push(gp.getValue('user'));
  }
}
```

By running the above code, we took down the calls from 3000 to 2, which in my eyes is really cool.

Forcing an update without updating

Sometimes you want to trigger e.g. the flow engine on a record to see if the condition now matches without needed to update the record itself. For this use there is a function called **setForceUpdate()** which you can use with the parameter **true** to trigger the engines without changing anything. In the example below I'm getting a record and then uses this function together with **update()**.

```
var sys = '8be0dc7ddb8ae7002288dc50cf96199f';
var getRITM = new GlideRecord('sc_req_item');
getRITM.get(sys);

getRITM.setForceUpdate(true);
getRITM.update();
```

If I run this in the **scripts – background** I will get this result which indicates that the record has been "updated" without me changing anything.

[0:00:00.112] Script completed in scope global: script

Script execution history and recovery available here

Operation	Table	Row Count
update	sc_req_item	1

*** Script: yes, BR runs: RITM0010010

Now, the negative part here is that when I run the script, it updates a few fields like **updated by** & **updated** to mention a few. And you probably don't want to have that. What you can add to the script is the function **autoSysFields()**. If you use that with the parameter **false** it will not update those fields for you. This can also be used when updating other fields and you don' want the system fields to be updated. Then the code will look like this and work just like we want it.

```
var sys = '8be0dc7ddb8ae7002288dc50cf96199f';
var getRITM = new GlideRecord('sc_req_item');
getRITM.get(sys);

getRITM.setForceUpdate(true);
getRITM.autoSysFields(false);
getRITM.update();
```

getEncodedQuery

This function is great to use if you have built a GlideRecord query through script and you want to see how the encoded query looks like from that build. In this example I have just a small query build in this example and notice that you don't need to use **query()** to be able to get the encoded version.

```
var getInc = new GlideRecord('incident');
getInc.addActiveQuery();
getInc.addQuery('priority', '1');

gs.debug(getInc.getEncodedQuery());
```

When I run the code in scripts – background I will get the following output.

[0:00:00.014] Script completed in scope global: script

Script execution history and recovery available here

*** Script: [DEBUG] active=true^priority=1

BUSINESS RULES

Business rules is server side code that runs when either someone/something queries the database. An example would be a user wanting to look at a list of incidents or a specific incident. Here the **Query** and **Before** business rules will run before the user sees the list or form. Then then business rules do nothing until the user submit/update the record and then another types of business rules are run.

Business rules are good to use for manipulating the query before the user sees the incident list, doing some additional changes to a record before it is saved in the database or even updating other records depending on the record that someone/something where updating. What you always shall keep in mind is that you should never use current.update() in a business rule, since it can lead to performance issues and eternal loops. You also have more configurable options when a Business rule should run, like on **Insert/Update/Delete** and of course you can setup specific conditions for it to run as well.

The steps are as following when a query is made to the database:
1. User/Machine/Script does a query

2. The Query Business rules run before the query hits the database

3. The Display Business rules run before for form/list etc. is displayed for the user.

4. Then it waits until the record(s) is being inserted, updated or deleted

5. The Before Business rules runs before the data is saved into the database.

6. The After Business rules runs after the data has been saved

123

7. The Async Business rules runs while the user can continue working.

Here is a deeper explanation about what kind of business rules there are and how/when they work.

Query Business Rule

This type of BR is used to modify the queries that are send to the database and this is before any data is collected, which means you can't do things like "0**if (current.active)**" since the BR have no idea what value current.active has. You pretty much use query BR to restrict what kind of data that the user can see. This is another way to restrict access from specific users unless they should be able to see it. Remember that comparing to ACL, a query business rule can only define if a user can see the whole record or not. Baseline there is a query business rule on the sys_user table which limits the result of the users to only active user if the user doesn't have the admin role. It looks like this:

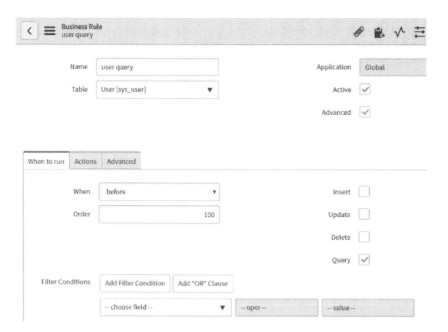

And you can see on the Advances tab is where the magic happens.

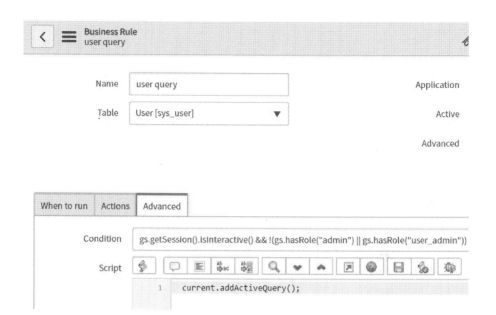

What will happen here is that if the user query the incident table and don't have the role **admin** or **user_admin**, it will add **current.addActiveQuery()** to the query and the user will only get back records that are active. In this case it also checks if it's a user that is doing the query with **gs.getSession().isInteractive()** through a form or similar and not e.g. a REST call. This is the reason why a normal user doesn't seen inactive users when they for example click on the caller field on incident. This business rule makes sure the user only sees active users.

There are a few limitations with **Query** business rules and one of the most important is that it doesn't support **NQ** (which is the top level of OR). Meaning when you have two sets of conditions. Here is a graphical example of it:

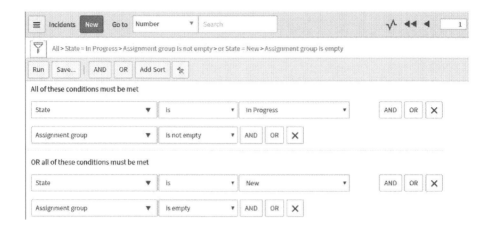

And when you turn this into an encoded query for the **Query Business rules** it will use the **^NQ** and the whole query will look like this when you copy it from the breadcrumb:

state=2^assignment_groupISNOTEMPTY^NQstate=1^assignment_groupISEMPTY.

Now when you use this in a query business rule it will probably work in the list view, and the reason is that you don't have any other conditions already set. If you had multiple query business rules active on the same table, this will freak those queries out as well and give you very strange behaviors. But it will really mess up when you try to access a single record since they run then as well. And when we want to look at a single record, we already have a query like **Number=INC000023**. Then it will just append the query business rule query on that and it will look like this **number=INC000023^state=2^assignment_groupISNOTEMPTY^NQstate=1^assignment_groupISEMPTY**.

Often you might run into the conversation about using before business rules instead of ACLs. This mostly since if you are limiting the records through ACL, you will in a list get say 300 records, but on the first page with you can only see 5 out of the 20 records on the page. The other 15 is restricting from your view. With a query business rule you will only get back records you can see and in this example on the first page all 20 records will be visible for you. In the picture below, the user should see in total 17 incidents, but on the first page with 20 records, he will only see 12 (all depends on how it's sorted).

Picture above is from the incident table where I actually deactivated the query business rule to get the behavior seen above.

Last thing about query business rules is that they don't affect database views. Meaning that if I have a query business rule on the incident table says it should only show active incidents. Then when I list incidents I don't see the closed incidents. But in a database view like **incident_sla** it ignores the query business rule on incident and shows incidents that are closed. If you want it to be only active on the database view as well, you will need to set a **query** business rule on the database view directly.

Display business rule

So what can we use the Display BR to? Well, if we know that we will need data that we want to use in a client script, but isn't available in the form. Then we can use the display BR to run server script and put the info in something called the g_scratchpad and then use it later in the client script. Just be careful, since it put the data in the scratchpad when the form is loading, that also means that if then the user doesn't do anything for like 10 min and the come back and edits something, the client script uses that data. It might be old and not correct. If you instead use an Ajax call, you will get "live" data for your client script. Here is an example of a display business rule script where it looks if the incident has any active child tasks. Then the client script will take this information and display it on the form when it's loading.

Example of display Business rule:

```
(function executeRule(current, previous /*null when
async*/) {
    g_scratchpad.activeTasks = 0;
    var countActiveTasks = new
GlideAggregate('incident_task');
    countActiveTasks.addEncodedQuery('active=true');
    countActiveTasks.addAggregate('COUNT');
    countActiveTasks.query();

    if (countActiveTasks.next()){
        g_scratchpad.activeTasks
=countActiveTasks.getAggregate('COUNT');
    }
}) (current, previous);
```

And then the onLoad client script:

```
function onLoad() {
    //Type appropriate comment here, and begin script below
    if (g_scratchpad.activeTasks > 0){
        g_form.addInfoMessage("There is " +
g_scratchpad.activeTasks + " incident tasks active on this
incident");

    }
}
```

Now when I got to an incident with at least 1 active incident task I get the message directly on my screen when the form is loaded.

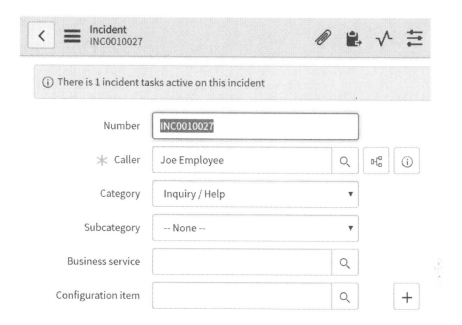

Before Business rule

This business rule hits before the data is saved into the database. But since the data hasn't been saved. Here we can modify fields like current.u_no_idea = 'bad imagination';

We can also use a before BR to validate the information to check if it should be allowed to be saved. Doing this here instead having a client script doing it. If the data isn't correct, you can abort the action with **current.setAbortAction(true)**. But be careful with aborting a save with this, since it will stop the insert and it will stop all **after** business rules. But it won't stop the rest of the **Before** business rules that are running on the record. You can do the same functionality with a **client script**, so evaluate your options before you decide how & where you want to implement this functionality to abort a save.

After business rule

Looking at the process you can see that the **After** business rules runs after the data has been saved to the database. Now is a perfect place to update other records beside the current one. Yes, you have access to the current object, but that is more to be able to use this data to do conditions and for example IF-statements to decide what other records to update.

This means that you shouldn't use an after business rule to update the current record. Since if you do, you will need to add a current.update() in your code and then all the "before" BR will run again, since we are trying to save/update something in the database... And again, is there anything in the current object we can't do in a before BR that we need to do in a after? I wouldn't say so.

Looking at all of the above, we are hitting user experience, making complex **After** business rules of any kind of the above will affect the user experience. Even an after business rule doesn't let the user do anything else until it's finished. And that leaves us to the last one.

Async business rule

Async business rule is something that needs more appreciation and could probably be used more often. Async (Asynchronous) is similar to after business rule but here it lets the user go and can do other stuff and put this on the "let's do it when we got time" list. If the condition on the Async business rule hits true, it understands that there is work to do and creates a schedule job to handle all that work. Its schedule to run immediately through the workers, but it doesn't guarantee when it's finished.

What's good to know that the business rule isn't run within the user's own active session, but when the schedule job is ready to go, it impersonate the user and a new session is created for this job. This will probably not have any affect, but can be good to know. So if you got things that needs to get updated after a record is saved and not in an extremely time critical way, Async is the way to go. There is one negative part about **Async** compare to an **After** business rule and that is that since the Async is thrown into the job queue, it doesn't longer have access to the previous record and its values. So that will restrict what you can do. For example you can't do a condition that checks "if state changes from" since it will only know what it changes to.

Business rules examples

I want to give you some good examples of what you can do with a business rule. I also tried to remember and give examples that I used in real requirements and hopefully can help you as well in the daily business. Some of these actually makes requirements very simple and will make you go from a chuck of code to no code at all.

Check if date field is within specific timeframe

This example can be used to check if for example a date field has a date that is in the past. I've seen many example of a good amount of code to do this, but basically you can solve this with a business rule and not even write a single line of code.

So the conditions would look like this:

And the **Action** section would be configured like this to abort the insert:

The Business rule above will only run if the field **Planned start date** is in the past and not empty. IF that is the case, it will abort the current save and give the user an message why it was aborted.

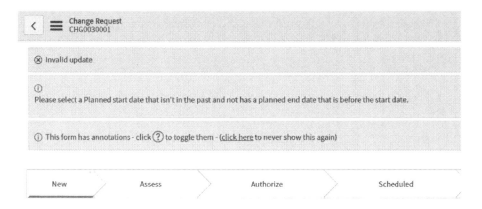

Copy one attachment from a record with many attachments

There might be times when you want to copy one attachment from a record, but not all of them. In that case this script might come in handy to use within a business rule in other places as well.

In this example we have the record **REQ0010012** where there are two attachments (testone & testtwo).

And we want to copy only testone.txt over to **REQ0010011**. What we can do then is use the following script.

```
var sourceTable = 'sc_request';
var sourceSysID =
'ac21d17edb4aab002288dc50cf9619fc';//Example REQ0010012

var getSource = new GlideRecord(sourceTable);
getSource.get(sourceSysID);

var fileName = 'testone'; //without file-extension
var getAttach = new GlideSysAttachment();
var attachContent = getAttach.get(getSource, fileName);

var targetTable = 'sc_request';
var targetSysID = '03725c7ddb8ae7002288dc50cf9619ce';//
Example REQ0010011
var getTarget = new GlideRecord(targetTable);
getTarget.get(targetSysID);

var copyAtt = new GlideSysAttachment();

copyAtt.write(getTarget, fileName, "text/plain",
attachContent);
```

What this does is that it gets the source record and get the specific attachment that we are looking for. Then we just write a new attachment the target record of our choice.

Validation against condition builder field

You might have requirements where you end up building functionality through a condition builder field. Just like you have business rules against a specific table, you can setup configuration records with a condition builder field and then through script take a record and see if it matches any of those condition records. And based on which record it matches, you can do different actions. In the example below, this script is running in a business rule that runs whenever a record is inserted into the specific table. It then takes the record (**current**) and matches it against my action records that has the condition builder field and see if it has any matches. More detailed explanation comes after the script.

```
(function executeRule(current, previous /*null when
async*/) {

    var findAction = new
GlideRecord('x_8294_aws_dash_action');
```

```
    findAction.addActiveQuery();
    findAction.query();

    while(findAction.next()){
        var match = GlideFilter.checkRecord(current,
findAction.condition, true);

        if(match){
            //Do what you to do when you have a match
            if (findAction.script){
                var evaluator = new
GlideScopedEvaluator();
                evaluator.evaluateScript(findAction,
'script');
            }
        }
    }
}) (current, previous);
```

Let's break down the code and see what it does:

In the first part you can see that first I'll go query all the active records in my table **x_8294_aws_dash_action**.

```
    var findAction = new
GlideRecord('x_8294_aws_dash_action');
    findAction.addActiveQuery();
    findAction.query();
```

Then I loop through the result and uses the **GlideFilter** functionality to match the current object with the condition field on my Action record. The last parameter is set to **True** so that if the condition has multiple conditions it needs to match them all to return **true**.

```
    while(findAction.next()){
        var match = GlideFilter.checkRecord(current,
findAction.condition, true);
```

If there then is a match the code inside **if(match)** will run. Here I have also added code so that if my action fields has a **Script** field just like e.g. business rules has. That script field is named **script** and if it finds that field, it will run that code.

```
    if(match){
        //Do what you to do when you have a match
        if (findAction.script){
```

```
                            var evaluator = new
GlideScopedEvaluator();

                        evaluator.evaluateScript(findAction,
'script');
                }
        }
```

Redirect to a different URI after save

The question normally surface now and then on the community on how to redirect in a business after an insert/update has been made. The requirements are often that you want to perhaps redirect to another record or maybe even redirect to a record that has been created. Remember that we are looking into how to redirect in a **Business Rule**, from e.g. a **UI Action** there are other recommendations. But when it comes to business rules it's recommend to use **gs.setRedirect()**. The other option is action.setRedirectURL() which is supposed to be used on UI Actions only, but it might work with business rules as well, but I have come into situations where it doesn't and I can't really find the answer of when it works and when it doesn't. So, it's better to always go for **gs.setRedirect()** in a business rule.

Another thing about redirect is that it will only work if the user press **Update**. If they press **Save** the redirect will not happen, no matter how much you are trying to do it in the script.

Create a csv file from a string

This is a script that I have found and kept as it might come in handy to use sometime and I really want to share it as well. So what this does it creates a string that is then uses to create a **CSV** file and attaches it to a record. I haven't had a use case for this exact script, but it has helped me solved certain other requirements that is touching this functionality.

```
    checkFieldUsage("table_to_check",
"fileName_without_extension", true, false);

    function checkFieldUsage(table, filename, usePercentage,
includeOOB) {

        if (!table || !filename) {
            return;
        }
        var rec = new GlideRecord("sys_user");
        rec.setLimit(1);
        rec.addQuery("sys_id", gs.getUserID());
        rec.query();
```

```
if (rec.next()) {
    var gr = new GlideRecord(table);
    gr.setLimit(1);
    gr.query();
    gr.next();
    var f = gr.getFields();
    var fieldLabels = [];

    var dataObj = {};

    for (var i = 0; i < f.size(); i++) {
        var fieldName = f.get(i).getName() + "";
        if (fieldName.indexOf("u_") != 0) {
            if (includeOOB) {
                fieldLabels.push(fieldName);
            }
        } else {
            fieldLabels.push(fieldName);
        }

    }

    csv = "Class," + fieldLabels.join(",") + "\n";


    var limit = fieldLabels.length;

    var ga = new GlideAggregate(table);
    ga.addAggregate("COUNT", "sys_class_name");
    ga.query();
    while (ga.next()) {
        var klass = ga.sys_class_name + "";
        dataObj[klass] = {};
        dataObj[klass]["total"] =
ga.getAggregate("COUNT", "sys_class_name");
    }


    var checkGr = new GlideRecord(table);
    checkGr.intialize();
    for (var x = 0; x < limit; x++) {
        var field = fieldLabels[x] + "";
        for (kl in dataObj) {
            dataObj[kl][field] = 0;

        }
        var ga = new GlideAggregate(table);
        ga.addAggregate("COUNT", "sys_class_name");
```

```
            //For  boolean fields check how many are
marked as true
            if (checkGr[field].sys_meta.type == -7) {
                ga.addQuery(field, true);


            }
            //for integer fields, check how many have a
value more than 0
            else if (checkGr[field].sys_meta.type == 4) {
                ga.addQuery(field, "!=", 0)

            } else {

                ga.addNotNullQuery(field);

            }
            ga.query();
            while (ga.next()) {

                var klass = ga.sys_class_name + "";

                if (!dataObj[klass]) {
                    dataObj[klass] = {};
                }
                if (usePercentage) {
                    var usage = ga.getAggregate("COUNT",
"sys_class_name");
                    var percent = (usage /
dataObj[klass].total) * 100;
                    dataObj[klass][field] = percent;
                } else {
                    dataObj[klass][field] =
ga.getAggregate("COUNT", "sys_class_name");
                }


            }

        }
        var csv = "Class,Total," + fieldLabels.join(",") +
"\n";

        for (k in dataObj) {

            csv += k + "," + dataObj[k].total;
            var fieldValues = [];
            for (var x = 0; x < limit; x++) {
                var field = fieldLabels[x] + "";
```

```
            fieldValues.push(dataObj[k][field]);
        }

        csv += "," + fieldValues.join(",") + "\n";

    }

        GlideSysAttachment().write(rec, filename + ".csv",
"text/csv", csv);
    }
}
```

Getting around with GlideDateTime

A common question on the community is how to handle different requirements that involves a **DateTime** field. It might be everything from getting the format right, to add a few days or to get which day in the week it is. There are also multiple solutions to this and most of them involves a rather large chunk of code. But, some of these requirements can easy be solved through baseline **GlideDateTime**, just give it a look and see what you can find. Here are a few examples of what you can do which requires minimal code.

Before we start with the examples, I just want to remind that when you are working with **DateTime**, it's very important to keep in mind that **getValue()** and get **getDisplayValue()** doesn't give you the same value. The getValue() gives you the date & time as if it was in the Instance Timezone. GetDisplayValue() on the other hand will show you the field value in the same timezone as the loggedin user. For most companies this won't be an issues since both the users and the instance will probably have the same timezone, but in some cases it can mess up some coding if not taking into account.

Convert Date format:
This is one way to convert a date format to fit into a **DateTime** field in servicenow. Here we get the date in a special way, but only with adding how it's setup we can actually just put into a variable the correct way:

```
    var date = '2018/12/02 21:23:45';
    var simpleDateFormat = 'yyyy/MM/dd HH:mm:ss';//Just define
how the date is setup

    var gdt = new GlideDateTime();
    gdt.setDisplayValue(date,simpleDateFormat);

    gs.debug("Date: " + gdt.getDisplayValue());
```

And this will give us:

[0:00:00.024] Script completed in scope global: script

Script execution history and recovery available here

*** Script: [DEBUG] Date: 2018-12-02 21:23:45

So just use the second parameter with **setDisplayValue()** to define what format the incoming data is.

Get which day a specific datetime is:

Another thing that comes around is that you want to get which day of the week a specific date is. This is also easy solvable through the **getByFormat()** function. In the example below we are figuring out which day the date in the resolved_at field is and which day it is today.

```
var getTodaysDate = new GlideDateTime().getDate();
gs.debug("Todays day: " +
getTodaysDate.getByFormat('EEEE'));

var getInc = new GlideRecord('incident');
getInc.get('e8caedcbc0a80164017df472f39eaed1');//just get
an incident.

var getDay = new
GlideDateTime(getInc.getDisplayValue('resolved_at')).getDate(
);
gs.debug("Resolved day: " + getDay.getByFormat('EEEE'));
```

And here is the result when you run the code:

[0:00:00.025] Script completed in scope global: script

Script execution history and recovery <u>available here</u>

```
*** Script: [DEBUG] Todays day: Sunday
*** Script: [DEBUG] Resolved day: Tuesday
```

<u>Just do something on weekdays:</u>

Then the requirement comes where you want to create something on specific weekdays and then nothing on the rest. For this you can use the **GlideDate()** to make the magic happen. In this case we want to do something on Mondays, Wednesdays and Fridays but nothing on the rest of the days.

```
var getDay= new GlideDate();

var day = getDay.getByFormat('EEEE');
if(day == 'Sunday' || day == 'Wednesday' || day ==
'Friday'){
//Do some magic
}
else {
//Do something else or nothing
}
```

SCRIPT INCLUDE

One of the beautiful things in ServiceNow for the developers are Script Includes. What most of us hate the most is to write the same code more than once. It all boils down to that if you write the same code more than once, turn it into a function instead. Now of course this might be a bit exaggerated and it might turn into an obsessive behavior, but it's mostly true. Placing reusable code in one place makes life easier when you in the future is going to administrate it or when you need to reuse the code somewhere else. And when it comes to run Server-side code and calling Server-side code from client scripts, **Script Include** is the way to go. Try to make more generic functions so you can reuse them for multiple purposes than to have very specific functions. Of course, it all depends on the situation, but give it an extra thought before you start writing it up. Another thing that you might want to do before you start writing your own code is to see if there already might be a **function/Script Include** that exists in the baseline configuration that you can use. I will go through both scenarios in the pages below to give you a good hit how to both extend/change Baseline functions without changing the baseline code and create from scratch.

If you have been around for a long time or accidently stumble over a Business Rule which is set to table Global then you see the earlier way of how to handle this functionality in ServiceNow. Before Script Includes existed, the functions were put in Global Business Rules instead. This because if you set the table to **Global**, this business rule will run on any tables. This is of course nothing that is recommended nowadays since it will become a major performance issue with all those business rules running on all the tables. Compare that to Script Includes which is only loaded.

Create Script Include from scratch

When you create your own Script Include you first need to decide where it's going to be used. Is it going to be used only on the Server-side code, only being called through a client script or perhaps even both ways? If you are going to use this through a client script, make sure you mark the **Client Callable** checkbox that is on the Script Include form.

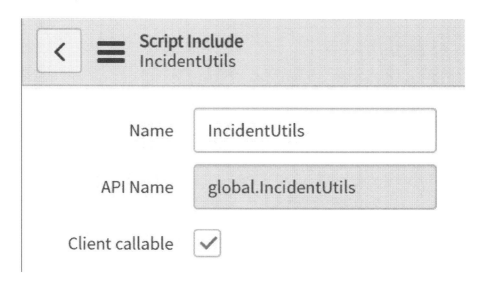

After that is just to start creating your own functionality. And to give you a good start, here is an example of a function that take the sys_id of a CI and returns the groups that is in the field **Support Group**. This script below is configured to work both with server-side scripting and through client-side and a **GlideAjax** call. I will go through part of the code further down. The code below is saved in a Script Include named **acmeClientScriptUtil** and it has the **Client Callable** field checked.

```
var acmeClientScriptUtil = Class.create();
acmeClientScriptUtil.prototype =
Object.extendsObject(AbstractAjaxProcessor, {
    /**
    * Gets the sys_id from the GlideAjax call and gets the
support group.
    *
    * @param {string} sys_id - sys_id of the record that is
sent through the GlideAjax call.
    * @return {JSON} a object containing both the value and
displayValue of the support group.
    */
    getSupportGrp: function(ci_sysid) {

            var ci = this.getParameter('syspam_ci_sysid')?
this.getParameter('syspam_ci_sysid') : ci_sysid;
```

```
            var returnGrp = {};
            var getCI = new GlideRecord('cmdb_ci');
            getCI.get(ci);

            if(getCI.support_group){
                    returnGrp.value =
getCI.getValue('support_group');
                    returnGrp.displayValue =
getCI.getDisplayValue('support_group');

                    return JSON.stringify(returnGrp);
            }
            else
                    return;
        },

    type: 'acmeClientScriptUtil'
});
```

To then use this functionality in a client script, I have put the following code in an **onChange** client script for the field **Configuration Item**. So, when it changes, it will get the support group from the CI and put that in the assignment group field.

```
    function onChange(control, oldValue, newValue,
isLoading, isTemplate) {
        if (isLoading || newValue === '') {
            return;
        }

        var ga = new GlideAjax('acmeClientScriptUtil');
        ga.addParam('sysparm_name', 'getSupportGrp');
        ga.addParam('syspam_ci_sysid', newValue);

        ga.getXML(assignGrp);

        function assignGrp(response){
            var answer =
JSON.parse(response.responseXML.documentElement.getAttribute(
"answer"));
            if(answer){
                g_form.setValue('assignment_group',
answer.value, answer.displayValue);
            }
        }
    }
```

In the code above, you can see I specify the name of the Script Include I'm calling with **acmeClientScriptUtils**. Then I define which function I want to call with **getSupportGrp** and for last, I send with the **newValue** which holds the sys_id of the new CI the user has put in the field. When I then get my response back and it holds a value (since not all CIs has a support group) I will put that value in the **assignment_group** field. Notice that not only set the sys_id of the group, but also the displayValue. This is to avoid another **Server Call** to get the group name. Since if you just put in a sys_id of a group, you will notice that suddenly the group name will show up. And that is because it went back to the server again to get the name. This can be avoided with setting the displayValue as well with the **g_form.setValue(fieldname, value, displayValue)**.

So that was how to use the **Script Include** in a client script. Now if we want to use the same functionality in server-side code you can do something like this.

```
var ci_sysid = '3a5dd3dbc0a8ce0100655f1ec66ed42c';//Just a
sys_id from a record in cmdb_ci table.

gs.debug(new
acmeClientScriptUtil().getSupportGrp(ci_sysid));
```

Which will give this result if you run it in e.g. **Scripts – Background**.

[0:00:00.041] Script completed in scope global: script

Script execution history and recovery available here

*** Script: [DEBUG] {"value":"8a5055c9c61122780043563ef53438e3","displayValue":"Hardware"}

And what you need to do to make it work in both places is not much, but it needs to be done. In my code it's all about these lines:

```
getSupportGrp: function(ci_sysid) {

        var ci = this.getParameter('syspam_ci_sysid')?
this.getParameter('syspam_ci_sysid') : ci_sysid;
```

When I use client-side code, I define the parameter with just this line:

```
ga.addParam('syspam_ci_sysid', newValue);
```

Then in the **Script Include** I use **this.getParameter('sysparm_ci_sysid')** to get the value in that parameter.

But when calling with server-side code I do like this:

```
new acmeClientScriptUtil().getSupportGrp(ci_sysid)
```

Where **ci_sysid** is the variable which has data of the sys_id. Now, to get this to work in a **Script Include** I need to define in in the function like this:

```
getSupportGrp: function(ci_sysid) {
```

Here I say that you can put in one parameter when you call the function and that value is stored in the variable ci_sysid which can be used in the function. The name ci_sysid can be pretty much anything, but try to keep good name standard, so it's easy for anyone else to understand you code. Now to make this work for both sides, we need to check if there is either a parameter sent with or the value is in the function call. This is where this line comes in.

```
var ci = this.getParameter('syspam_ci_sysid')?
this.getParameter('syspam_ci_sysid') : ci_sysid;
```

This says that if **this.getParameter('sysparm_ci_sysid')** exists, then that is the value the variable ci will get. Otherwise it will get the value of the variable ci_sysid. This is a good functionality to keep in your **Client Callable** Script Includes, since you never know when you suddenly needs the same function on the Server-side as well.

Extend to change or add functionality in existing SI

There a lot of baseline Script Includes which has really good functionality and for quite a few releases ServiceNow has made is easy for us to add or change existing functionality in some of the Script Includes. Let me explain on how that is being done. In my example I will use the two script includes called **KBKnowledgeSNC** which is a read only Script Include protected by the "protection policy". Which also has been improved. Earlier you could easy change record with protection policy set to **Read Only** just by downloading the record as xml, do the changes and then import it again. Now this isn't possible anywhere is quite good and also shows that reporting things like this to **HI** is worth it's time to get a better product.

But let's get back to the Script Includes. **KBKnowledgeSNC** is filled with many functions that you can use. In this case ServiceNow has also created the other Script Include that we are going to use, and it's called **KBKnowledge**. You might see a pattern on at least the newer records that the **Read Only** version has **SNC** in the end of the name. Let's take a closer look at the Script Include **KBKnowledge**.

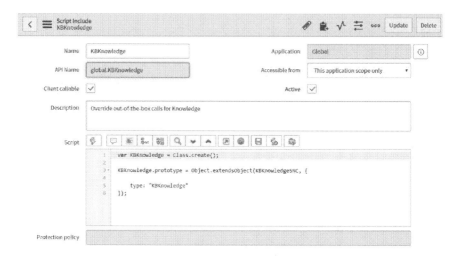

As you can see it's just an empty shell, ready at your disposal to be modified. You can see at line 3 in the script that is extends the Script Include **KBKnowledgeSNC**:

```
KBKnowledge.prototype =
Object.extendsObject(KBKnowledgeSNC, {
```

This means that if you use this Script Include in your code, it will have access to all the functions that exists in **KBKnowledgeSNC** as well. This actually goes a bit deeper since **KBKnowledgeSNC** is extended from the Script Include **KBCommon** (Which extends **KBCommonSNC**). Especially when you troubleshoot, keep an eye on this structure so you know where to look to find the specific functionality you are looking for. Here is an example how we can use this "empty" Script Include and still call for a function that exists in **KBCommon**.

```
var x = new KBKnowledge().getKnowledgeRecord('KB0011057');

gs.debug(x.getValue('short_description'));
```

will give the result:

Script execution history and recovery available here

*** Script: [DEBUG] Create an IT ticket to rebuild the device

You can see that here I pass in the article number and get in return the GlideObject of the knowledge article. What happen is that it goes down the hierarchy of Script Includes until it finds the function and then runs it. This means that if I would define the function **getKnowledgeRecord()** in **KBKnowledge** it will not go deeper down and find the original function in the Script Include **KBCommonSNC**. Let's try this and see how it works. We need to add the function to the Script Include **KBKnowledge** and modify it. In this example I will just force it to return a specific article to show you how to use it. Then it's up to your imagination of what you can do with this.

```
var KBKnowledge = Class.create();

KBKnowledge.prototype =
Object.extendsObject(KBKnowledgeSNC, {

    getKnowledgeRecord: function(articleNumber){

                var gr = new GlideRecord('kb_knowledge');
                gr.addQuery('number', 'KB0011056');
                gr.query();
                if (gr.next())
                        return gr;
                else
                        return false;

    },

    type: "KBKnowledge"
});
```

Now you can see that after my change it will always return the article with number **KB0011056**. Testing it now shows that is works as we wanted:

```
var x = new KBKnowledge().getKnowledgeRecord('KB0011057');

gs.debug(x.getValue('number'));
```

and you can see that even if we specified article **KB00110057**, we got returned **KB00110056**.

> [0:00:00.020] Script completed in scope global: script

> Script execution history and recovery <u>available here</u>

> *** Script: [DEBUG] KB0011056

We can still use the original function by calling a Script Include further down the hierarchy like this:

```
var x = new
KBKnowledgeSNC().getKnowledgeRecord('KB0011057');

gs.debug(x.getValue('number'));
```

Just remember that there might be Baseline code that is already calling the Script Include **KBKnowledge** so make sure you know what you are doing when you change Baseline functionality and don't forget to test everything that can be affected by your changes before it hit production.

Useful baseline Script includes

There are quite a few baseline Script Includes that you might not think of and start inventing your own. So before (just like with everything else in ServiceNow) starting to build your own functionality. Take a look around in the instance, docs and community to make sure there isn't anything you can use or copy for your requirements. If you go to the Script Include table in your instance, I would take a look at the ones you can see there e.g. that ends with **Util(s)**. They probably have some nice features for you to use. Then there are of course others like the **KBKnowledge** which I used in my examples above. I stumbled over that one myself when I was configuring the Knowledge process for a client.

Here are a few examples of Script Includes that I think is very useful in some circumstances. You can search for them on docs to get more information about the functions they have:

- **JSUTIL:** got a few common functionalities that is used within JavaScript. I myself really like the **logObject()** which easily gives you more information about a GlideObject than the famous **[object GlideRecord]**.

- **GlideRecordUtil:** A class that doesn't have so many functions, but what it has is really nice. One function is the **getFields()** which returns an array of all field labels for a **GlideRecord**.

- **GlideSecureRandomUtil:** Also a class that doesn't have that many functions. But nice to use if you want to create some random long strings, integers and so on.

WORKFLOWS

It feels like workflows have been around here forever and I can honestly say that I have no clue if workflows are something that has been there from the very beginning or are something that was invented on the way. It has always been there since I stepped into the ServiceNow world. But I think I will be around when it will not be in ServiceNow anymore. **Flow** (designer) stepped up on the scene in the Kingston release and just have taken up more and more space in **London and Madrid** releases. I think that we are looking at the "Workflow killer". But since Workflow is so used everything, it will take a long time until it's been 100% phased out, if it ever will be. There is quite a few old functionalities that you wonder why they still are around, but have been used by so many customers that it's hard to remove it. But I doubt that we will see any new functionality being developed for workflow and one of the reasons is **IntegrationHUB** which doesn't work with Workflow and will replace **Orchestration**. I will not spend too much time with workflows, but I have some tips and tricks that I would like to share.

First of all, make sure you have workflows that properly end and get state Complete. If you build workflows that never reach the end activity, you have a disaster waiting to happen. Most common is that you haven't thought of all the options the fulfiller/end user can take in a process and somehow the record is complete, but the workflow is stuck at an activity waiting to get to the next activity. One example I ran into was around the normal change workflow. We were using the Baseline workflow and after a while we decided to make it a bit simpler. This ended up in that we removed a state, rebuild the workflow and were happy. All new changes worked like a charm. But what you have to remember with workflows is that even if I publish a new workflow, all the older ones that already are executing are still running by the old version. So, in this case, in the older versions, we needed that state that was now active. So, we couldn't easily close those already existing workflows without tweaking. I normally say when I'm teaching about workflows that you can compare it to a house blueprint. The architect for the house draws a nice blueprint for you and when you are done, you send a copy (context) of this blueprint to the construction workers which start to build your house. Then another customer comes to the architect and looks at the blueprint. They really like it but change a few things. Now they send this copy (context) to their construction workers which start to build that house. But of course, your house is still going to be built by your version of the blueprint. This is how the workflow versions work as well. When you make changes and publish them, only new workflow contexts will have the new version. The older already existing contexts will still be running on the older version. Besides that, here are a few "good to know" things I stumbled over.

How to reset workflow

Sometimes you end up with the requirements that you want to reset a workflow and let it start all over again. There is a Baseline Business Rule that you can use which is called SNC Approval – Reset Conditions. This Business Rule is running on the change_request table, so if you want to use this on any other tables, you can pretty much copy and paste most of the code to get it to work. Let us take a little deeper look into the script and see what it does and how we can utilize it.

```
    // these are the conditions under which the change request
approvals need to be cancelled and reset
    // steps to activate
    // 1. enable this business rule
    // 2. add some comments so the reset will be noted in the
approval history
    // 3. uncomment the code for restart or reset based on
your requirements
    // 4. define the reset condition in checkResetConditions
function below
    // 5. you must set doReset once you capture the change(s)
you are interested in


    var comment = '';  //written to the approval_history
    if (checkResetConditions()) {

        // create a global variable lock on the current record
        // this will prevent triggering a second reset while
the first reset is still in progress
        // lock will be release in a late running business rule
called 'Workflow Release Lock'
        chg_wf_lock = new GlideRecordLock(current);
        chg_wf_lock.setSpinWait(50);   //wait for lock
        if (chg_wf_lock.get()) {
```

```
        gs.print('SNC Approval conditions business rule is
locking the ' + current.getDisplayValue() + ' during the
workflow reset');

        // The following options are available for resetting
the approvals:
        //
        // 1. Mark all existing approvals for the change as
'cancelled' and restart the workflow to create new approvals
        //        new
WorkflowApprovalUtils().cancelAll(current, comment);
        //        new Workflow().restartWorkflow(current);
        //
        // 2. Delete all of the existing approvals for the
change and restart the workflow to create new approvals
        //        new WorkflowApprovalUtils().reset(current,
comment);
        //        gs.addInfoMessage('Workflow has been reset
since key fields have been modified');
        //
        // 3. Leave the approvals for the change in their
current state and restart the workflow.
        //     (so that any new approvals that are required
will be created)
        //        if (comment)
        //
current.setDisplayValue('approval_history', comment);
        //        new Workflow().restartWorkflow(current,
true);
        //


    }
  }

  function checkResetConditions() {

      var doReset = false;   //default to no reset
      //add reset conditions here such as:
      //if (current.assigned_to.changes())
        //doReset = true;   //enable the reset
      //
      return doReset;
  }
```

As you can see, the code itself has very good comments in it and it's easy to understand what you need to do. It uses the **restartWorkflow()** function to reset and it also gives you a couple of options as well when it comes to how to handle the approvals. You can reset it and leave the approvals be, so they don't need to approve the record again or you can of course also create new approvals if you wish. And you make your choice by removing the code lines for that specific choice in the business rule script above.

How to cancel a workflow

Now that we talked about how to restart a workflow, how about cancel a workflow. Sometime you need to cancel it with script because of certain requirements. In this example below, we run this code in a **Business Rule** and if you are running this somewhere else, you might need to replace the current **GlideObject** with the GlideObject which I have done here on the first three lines. Then I have also specified in the code which **Workflow Version** I want to cancel, since a record could have multiple workflows running and without this, I would get all of them.

```
//These three lines are just for an example and needed
since I didn't have a current object
    var currentSys = '8ecd7552db252200a6a2b31be0b8f581';
    var current = new GlideRecord('change_request');
    current.get(currentSys);

    var getWorkflowContext = new GlideRecord("wf_context");

    getWorkflowContext.addQuery("id",
current.getUniqueValue());
    //Remember to go in and change this to the correct
workflow_version of the flow you wan to cancel
    getWorkflowContext.addQuery("workflow_version",
"2633b949cb020200d71cb9c0c24c9c1d");
    getWorkflowContext.query();

        //If we find the context, cancel it.
    if (getWorkflowContext.next()) {

        var workflow = new Workflow();
        workflow.cancelContext(getWorkflowContext);
    }
```

Remember that if you want to cancel multiple workflows connected to the same record, you will need to do a **While loop** instead of an **IF-statement** at the end.

Testing with timers in the workflow

Timers can be used to a lot of things is the workflow. For example, to handle the SLA notifications where we want to wait for 50% of the time until breach and then send a notification and that is totally fine. The testing issue arises when you are building a workflow with timers and want to test it. Let's continue with the example of the SLA workflow, how can I test that it actually sends an email after 50% of the SLA time? I have seen many different suggestions like e.g. you change the duration on the SLA just to breach it, but that is kind of bending the rules of the testing. But what you can do is to manipulate when the timer triggers. So how does workflow timer work? When the workflow reaches a timer, it creates a scheduled job which gets **Next action** set to that date and time that the workflow is supposed to move to the next activity. Then the workflow just sits and waits to get a **Timer event** which is how it knows it's time to move from the timer activity to next activity in the workflow. In this example, I have created an incident, got a baseline P2 SLA to trigger. I have gone past the first "Wait 50% timer" now waiting for the next timer.

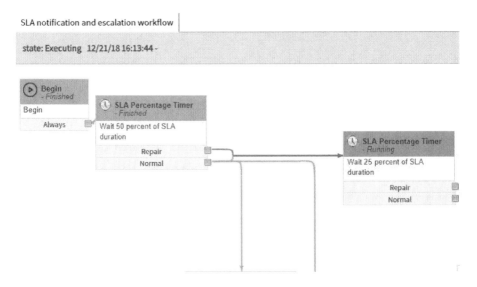

If I look in the table **Schedule (sys_trigger)** I can see my work is at the top. You can see it with the naming **Workflow + the sys_id of workflow context.**

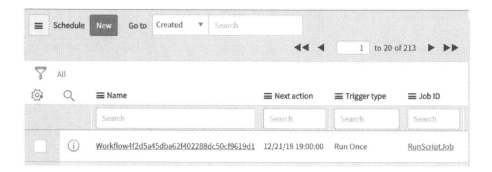

Worth remembering that in earlier releases and I'm not sure when it changed, but then it was named **WFTimer + sys_id**. After you find the scheduled job, you can just adjust the value in **Next action** to a bit closer your time and it will run and the timer activity in the workflow will be complete and the workflow will move to the next activity. Since you can do this manually, you can of course do it with scripting as well, but I don't really see any use for it considering you will only do this for testing and nothing you would need in production. And I hope you will be done with testing before you feel that you are doing this so much that you need a script to do it.

Branches and join

If you have used branch to create parallel activities remember to have a join after those activities. If you don't have it and have something that might look like this:

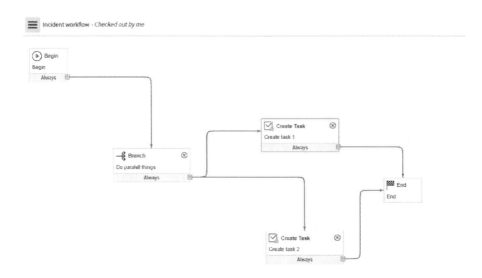

Then one task will be complete and move to the end. When that happens, the other task will automatically be cancelled. To stop this from happening, you should put a "join" after the parallel tasks. Then it will wait for them to be complete and then move to done.

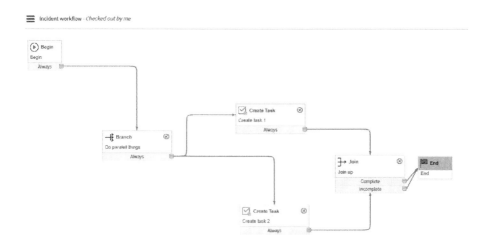

Also remember that when using branch/join, always make sure that the same amount of lines coming out from branch should go into the join activity. It doesn't matter where they come from or how many that are blue, as long as they are "connected" to it, it counts. If the amount isn't the same, it will count it as incomplete.

Nudge the workflow

Sometimes a workflow stops at an activity and you can't really understand why it did that. Everything seems ready when you look at the conditions for it to move forward, but something has happened, and it doesn't. I doubt you are the only one it has happened to and will not be the last one either. And at least when looking at the history it has happened so many times that there is a **Baseline UI Action** called just **Nudge** which is visible on the **Workflow context (wf_context)** table.

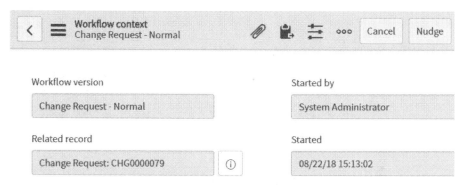

Clicking on this will simulate an update to the workflow and it will reevaluate the conditions for the activity it is currently on. I have used this functionality just a handful of times and it has solved a few of them. If you are having some issue with a specific workflow context and it doesn't want to move, I encourage you to try this and see if it works.

FLOW DESIGNER

Flow designer came to the ServiceNow world in Kingston. It didn't take up much attention but has quickly grown to be the future king of flow/workflows in my eyes. In Kingston it was mainly there for one functionality and that was to start the dawn of taking over **Async** Business Rules and scheduled jobs. Then in London we got new features like the ability of connecting flows to **Service Catalog Items** and having **SubFlows**. Then in Madrid we got for example reusable Actions through the **Flow API** which gives you both the option to call the actions from any scripts as well as start flows from scripting.

I have been playing around with it before it came for Kingston and I like it a lot. I see a bright future for this and it will or even has stepped up and taken over the workflow throne for just workflows. Keep in mind that also the **IntegrationHUB** is using flows and is also the new version of **Orchestration**. Both Workflows will probably be around for quite a few more releases, but I doubt anything new will be developed for them, for new fun things, it's all **Flow Designer** and **IntegrationHUB**. The reason we will be seeing it around for quite some time is more that is used in so many places now at customers and it will take quite some time to move all those functionalities into the new applications. When we talk about this move, I would recommend doing the move when you either are going to evolve into newer functionality/requirements or bug fixing. If it works in Workflow and Orchestration, let it be. There are other things that you can do and spend your time on than this move that will not give the business any new functionality to use.

I mention **Flow API** as a new feature in Madrid, but let's look more at what Madrid has to offer in the Flow Designer.

Flow Properties

Before Madrid, all flows ran as what you can call the system user. Now in Madrid the security has been tightened up and now you can set an option to change this to the user who initialized the session. This is done when you create the flow with the **Run As** option.

Flow Properties

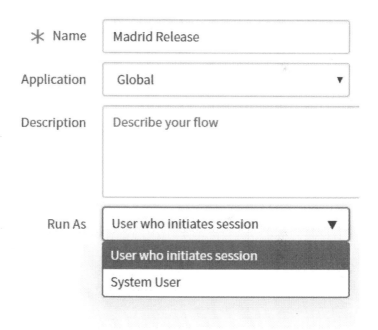

If you later would like to change this, you can do this through the flow properties button which you find in the upper right of the canvas.

New functions in Madrid for Trigger

In earlier releases, you could define in the trigger when to run (Created/Updated, Scheduled or Service Catalog) and that is the same in Madrid as well. What has changed is the **Run Trigger**. Earlier the choices you had were just **Once** or **Always**. Meaning that either you trigger the flow once per record or repeat it if the conditions match. For Madrid these have changed into new choices.

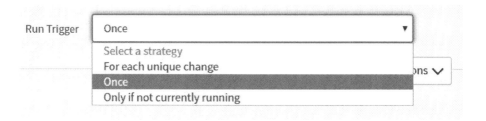

As you can see **Once** is still there, but the choice **Always** has been replaced with two new options which give you greater flexibility on when you want the flow to trigger.

Besides this, there is also now **Advanced Options** you can click on to get more setting to use.

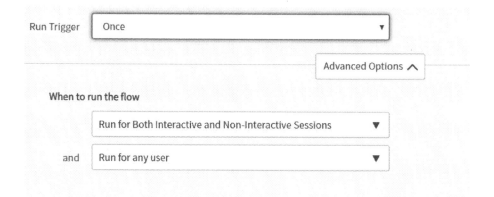

From here you can configure if the flow should run only in interactive sessions, non-interactive sessions or both. A good way to set it up if you for example want to trigger a flow only when a user is updating a record or only when an incoming REST call updates a record.

You can also configure so the flow only runs for specific people. Either through selecting those people who are allowed or those who isn't. And of course, there is an option for all users as well. I'm hoping to see User Criteria or something similar in future releases.

Flow logics

There have showed up a few more **Flow Logic** options than what existed before. Here is a nice picture of what you can find and use in Madrid.

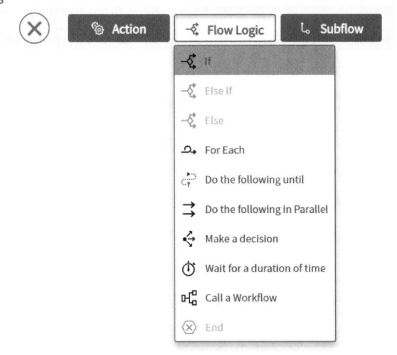

Here you can see that now you can make parallel actions in a flow and even call a workflow. With the **Call a Workflow** option, you can build new flows that leverage the existing workflows that you already have created and might still want to use until you rebuild them as a flow.

Branch and Join

One thing that still is missing in Madrid release is how to handle the **Branch & Join**. With that I can e.g. create 3 parallel tasks and when all of those are complete, I want the last task to be created. It can look like something like this::

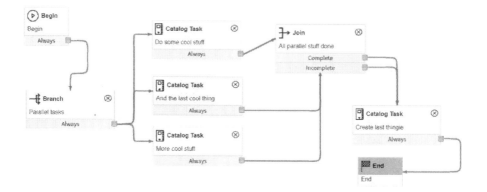

Now, this is a bit harder to create the same in Flow. But it's possible even if we still don't have the simple solution for this. If I would build the above functionality in a flow, I would do it something like this.

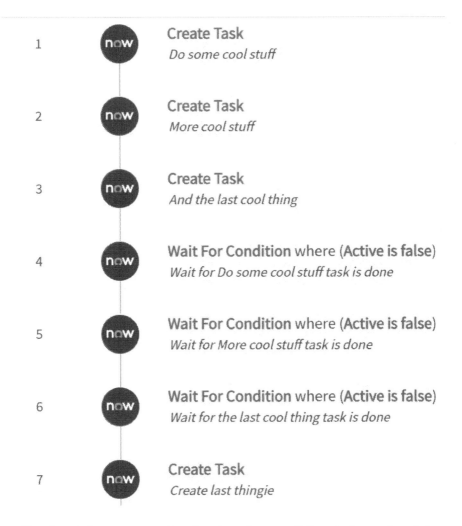

1	now	**Create Task** *Do some cool stuff*
2	now	**Create Task** *More cool stuff*
3	now	**Create Task** *And the last cool thing*
4	now	**Wait For Condition** where (**Active is false**) *Wait for Do some cool stuff task is done*
5	now	**Wait For Condition** where (**Active is false**) *Wait for More cool stuff task is done*
6	now	**Wait For Condition** where (**Active is false**) *Wait for the last cool thing task is done*
7	now	**Create Task** *Create last thingie*

Here I needed to create 3 wait actions to make sure all three tasks are done before moving on to the last task. So, it's possible, but requires a bit more thinking before setting it up.

I mention the Parallel flow logic earlier and let's look at how that can be used as well. In this example we have the workflow version which looks like this:

164

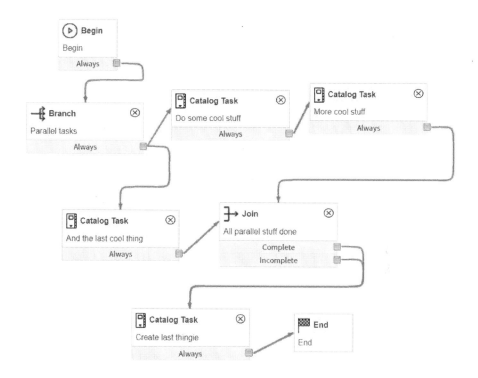

Here you can see that the branch goes out to two flows and the top flow has 2 activities in a sequential order and the other flow only has one activity before they both join together in the join activity. Now let's make the same logic in the flow designer.

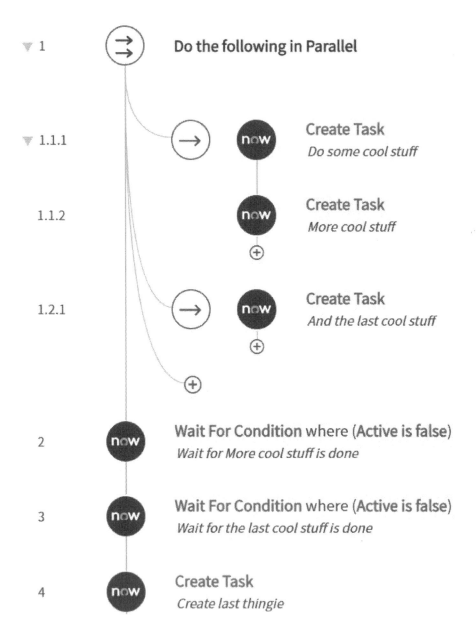

Here you can see we take use of the new Flow Logic **Do the following in Parallel** to make it work as we want. We also now only need to have two wait conditions in the end since as we already have wait for completion on the sequential line, we can set the wait condition for the last action only.

Custom Action and Action API

One thing that is really nice and I want to put some thoughts into is the **Custom Action** and its **Action API**. Flow designer is really going with the **"Pro-Code, Low-Code & No-Code"** vision in how to do things. And custom actions are a brilliant functionality to use this. With Custom Actions the Pro-code people can create your own actions with script, multiple steps and inputs/outputs. When this is done, the Low-Code & No-code (and of course Pro-code) can reuse those actions in their own fields. I think this will happen more often now in the earlier releases where flow designer is around, since it will take some time for ServiceNow to build all those wanted Baseline Actions. A good example is having the ability to copy an attachment from a record to another one. I built a Custom Action for this in London for a fellow community member, but in the Madrid release, attachment handling has four actions for different requirements you might has like copy or perhaps move an attachment.

Now for the **Action API** which takes the use of Action to a totally different level. With the Action API you can call and use an action from anywhere in the system where you can do scripting. I can see this as Script Include version 2.0. Just keep in mind that Madrid is the first release for the Action API and I bet we will see much improvement for it in the coming releases.

The flow designer also gives you good examples how to call the specific flow from both Server- & Client-side script. For this example, we have a flow that is made to trigger on the Incident table when Priority is 3. In the simple flow we then just create an incident task which is connected to the incident.

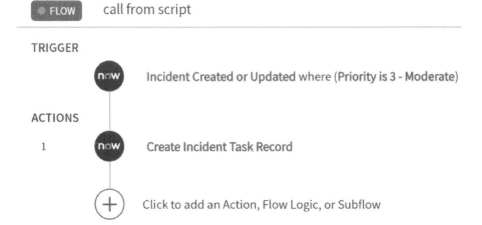

Now if we want to sometimes trigger this on another incident without changing the condition or perhaps it's hard to setup the condition correctly since it only uses the condition builder and there might be requirements that are too complex for that. So, to get the code to activate this flow we just click on the ellipsis menu and choose Code Snippet.

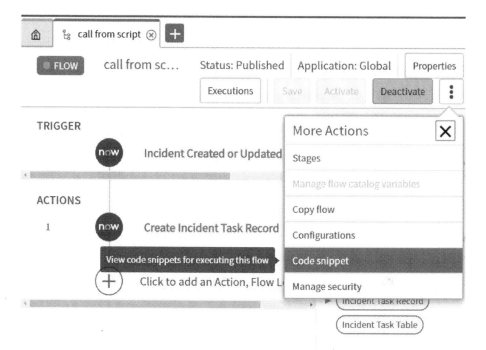

If Code Snippet is grayed out, make sure you have setup the **Trigger, Saved** and **Activated** it at least once. Then you should be able to choose it and see this modal:

Code Snippet To Execute This Flow

| Server | Client |

```
1   (function() {
2
3       try {
4           var inputs = {};
5           inputs['current'] = ; // GlideRecord of table:
6           inputs['table_name'] = 'incident';
7
8           // Start Asynchronously: Uncomment to run in background.
9           // sn_fd.FlowAPI.startFlow('global.call_from_script', inputs);
10
11          // Execute Synchronously: Run in foreground.
12          sn_fd.FlowAPI.executeFlow('global.call_from_script', inputs);
13
14      } catch (ex) {
15          var message = ex.getMessage();
16          gs.error(message);
17      }
18
19  })();
```

Start flow from server-side code

In the picture above, you can see the Server code which has both the option for the Asynchronous call with **.startFlow()** and Synchronous with **.executeFlow()**. On line 5 you give the GlideObject of the record that you want to run it on. Remember it needs a **GlideObject** and not just a sys_id. Here is an example where I call it from a Business Rule and just insert the **Current** as the GlideObject:

```
var inputs = {};
inputs['current'] = current; // GlideRecord of the record
you want to to use:
inputs['table_name'] = 'incident';// Name of the table the
record belongs to

sn_fd.FlowAPI.startFlow('global.call_from_script',
inputs);
```

Start flow from client-side code

To be able to call a flow from the client side, you first need to activate it (just like on Script Includes) and configure the security around it. So, let's take a look and see how that is done. To get to security, you click on the same ellipsis menu as for **Code Snippet** and then select **Manage Security** that is just below Code Snippet. And this modal will show up for you..

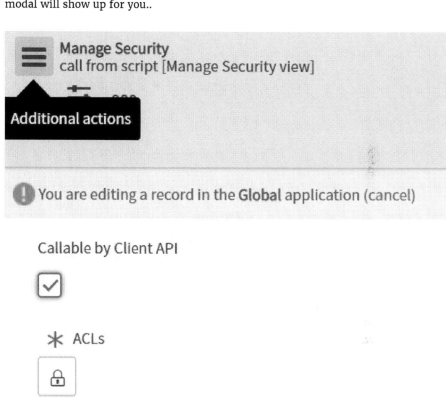

When you select **Callable by Client API**, another field shows up called **ACLs**. This is the security where you need to define an ACL for who is allowed to call this flow. This is something that is recommended with Client Callable Script Includes as well. So, before we are selecting anything here, let's create the ACL for our flow. It's a simple ACL with type **client_callable_flow_object** and when you select that it will automatically set Operation to **execute**. On the name field, you specify the database name of the flow and then set the conditions like a normal ACL.

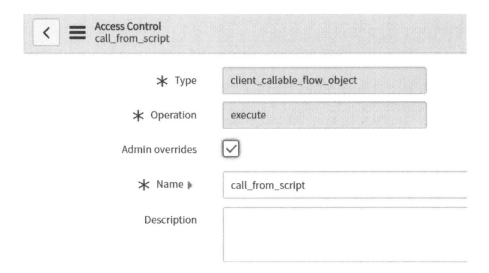

After this is done, you can go back to **Code Snippet** and click on the **Client** button to get the code you can use in a client script.

Code Snippet To Execute This Flow

Server	Client

```
1  (function() {
2
3      var inputs = {};
4
5      inputs['current'] = { // GlideRecord
6          table : '',
7          sys_id :
8      };
9      inputs['table_name'] = 'incident';
10
11      GlideFlow.startFlow('global.call_from_script', inputs)
12
13  })();
```

Learn more about API access to Flow Designer ⓘ

I have taken the code above and just pasted it into an onChange Client script to see that it works.

```
function onChange(control, oldValue, newValue, isLoading,
isTemplate) {
    if (isLoading || newValue === '') {
        return;
    }
        var inputs = {};

    inputs['current'] = { // GlideRecord
        table : 'incident',
        sys_id :  g_form.getUniqueValue()
    };
    inputs['table_name'] = 'incident';

    GlideFlow.startFlow('global.call_from_script',
inputs);
    }
```

You can see that I added the code to get the sys_id of the current record as well the tablename on the lines with:

```
table  :  'incident',
sys_id :   g_form.getUniqueValue()
```

and then the flow is running as it should.

Execute an Action outside of a flow

With the Madrid release it's now also possible to execute an Action outside of the flow. And here is where it basically starts to fill the same functionality as a script include. This works almost the exact same way as on flows. You can execute it both on client side and server side. If you want more details how to setup the client side ACLs etc. I recommend going through how to configure it for a flow which I described in the section above.

One big difference with executing an **Action** is how you do it. Either with Asynchronously (**startAction()**) or Synchronously (**ExecuteAction()**).

Code Snippet To Execute This Action

```
     Server   Client

1    (function() {
2
3        try {
4            var inputs = {};
5            inputs['ah_task'] = ; // GlideRecord of table: task
6
7            // Start Asynchronously: Uncomment to run in background. Code snippet will not have access to outputs.
8            // sn_fd.FlowAPI.startAction('global.wd_-_create_incident', inputs);
9
10           // Execute Synchronously: Run in foreground. Code snippet has access to outputs.
11           var outputs = sn_fd.FlowAPI.executeAction('global.wd_-_create_incident', inputs);
12
13           // Get Outputs:
14           // Note: outputs can only be retrieved when executing synchronously.
15           var Incident = outputs['Incident']; // Document ID
16
17       } catch (ex) {
18           var message = ex.getMessage();
19           gs.error(message);
20       }
21
22   })();
```

As it described in the code, if you run the code synchronously you will have access to the outputs from the Action. You won't have access to outputs from the Action if you run the code asynchronously. Sometimes it matters, sometimes it doesn't. So, keep in mind which is needed through the requirements and see this is another tool in your box with Display Business Rules and GlideAjax calls in Client scripts.

CLIENT SIDE CODING

Client side coding involves writing code mainly in places like Client Scripts, UI Policies, Catalog Client Scripts and Catalog UI Policies. It's also one of the areas where you can easily find solutions for the requirements that are asked from the business. But that doesn't mean that it's the best way to do it. I think almost everyone starts out here and solves things and then the more knowledge you get, the more things you will configure or customize in places to get better performance or solutions. Then again, some things work like a charm here as well.

One thing that you must keep in mind is that it's called **client side coding** because the code is running on the client's computer. This also means that depending on the internet connection, computer specifications, etc. it might run fast or really slow. The main reason for trying to have as little as possible as "Client Side" is that "Server Side" will always have better performance since that code is running on high performance hardware and doesn't need to go through the internet to get information from the database and so on.

When we do client side coding, Baseline you only have access to a more limited number of APIs to use compared to server side coding and another important thing is that you will only have access to the data that is on the fields that are shown on the form. A field can be hidden on the form but still accessible through coding. But this also mean that if you, for example, don't have the field "active" on the form, you can write code to check what value it has. Then you need to query the server to get that information. You can't dot-walk and e.g. get the assignment group's manager. For this, you also need to query the server for information. This is where your performance issues might start to show up.

It's so easy to go down this road and solve it fast through a client script but like every other place in ServiceNow, there are many ways to do things and Client Side Coding isn't an exception. Also keep in mind that it's been around for a long time and there are even Baseline configurations that might have been working as best practice when it was created, but it hasn't been updated with newer functionality and can fool you on what is the correct way when you create your own code.

For this I have two examples involving GlideRecord calls and using **getReference()** which today isn't recommended by ServiceNow and definitely not with their best practice.

Here is a Baseline example of a client script using a GlideRecord Call and it was created in 2013.

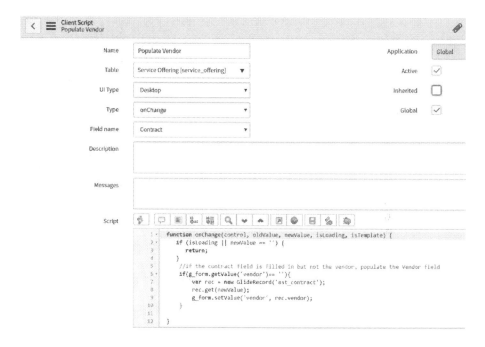

And here is a Baseline example of using **g_form.getReference()** which was created way back in 2009.

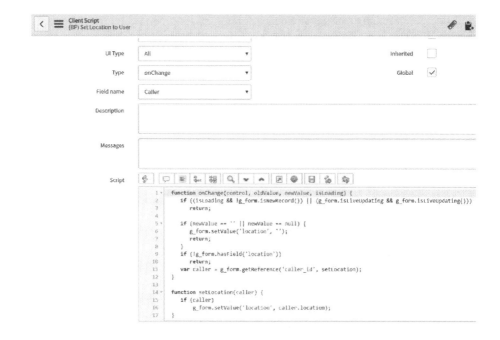

Now, first of all, this works but the main issue here is performance since both ways are retrieving the whole record while you in 99% of the cases only need one or two fields from the record. Often, the examples above are used since it's easy and doesn't require more than a line or two of code to get it done. But try to have the bigger picture in your head, since a single client might not cause any big difference in performance, but when you start to add them up, trouble will be showing up on the horizon. A single client script can easily mess up loading time for a form to 10+ seconds.

Before we go deeper into testing, I just want to mention the **JavaScript Executor** that you can use to run client-side code. If you are using Windows, you can press **Shift+Ctrl+Alt+J** and a modal will appear.

In here you can write and test client side code which can be very useful in testing or when you are troubleshooting.

OldValue & newValue

One thing that I have stumbled over and scratched my head before understanding it is how the **oldValue** and **newValue** works in client scripts. An onChange Client Script can be triggered multiple times before the user saves the record. If you do a comparison in the code with oldValue and newValue keep in mind that oldValue isn't the value that the field had before you changed it the second time, it is the value that the field had when the form was loaded. This means that the value it has is the same value it has in the database. I helped a community member with just this issue. He was looking at oldValue and if it wasn't all lowercase, he would turn it into all lowercase and insert that into the form with **g_form.setValue()**. But since he did that, he triggered the onChange script again and since it was looking at the oldValue, it triggered the change again and there was an infinite loop.

Using g_scratchpad

One way to get data from the server to the client side code is using what ServiceNow calls the g_scratchpad. With this, you can use a display business rule to put information into the scratchpad and then you can read the scratchpad in the client side code.

A good thing about this is that the user won't notice any delay when the page has loaded and is doing something on the form that makes the code execute since the code already has all the information and doesn't need to wait for a server lookup to get the data. Depending on how complex the code is, it might take a longer time to load the form since the display business rule is executed before the form is loaded.

What can turn out to be negative about this approach is that the data in the scratchpad can be old and not accurate anymore. Let's say you want to know the assignment group manager on the incident. If you do the lookup on a display business rule you can run at least two problems:

1. The group will change on the record before the client script is being triggered. This means that the lookup that was done in the display business rule was doing it on the wrong group and probably will have the wrong data.

2. Group don't change, but someone else was editing the group record and after the display business rule had ran, the manager was changed for that group. This also means that the scratchpad has the old manager as data.

Both scenarios above can lead to tickets taking longer time, wrong people get information and so on.

I would recommend using this method if you are getting data that isn't changing so often. The example above might be in the grey zone, since hopefully the group's manager doesn't change that often, but it was more used to demonstrate what to think of.

So, the scratchpad is used by giving it different variables and value. For example: **g_scratchpad.email** or **g_scratchpad.language**.

Example of the setup:

In the display Business rule, you will have:

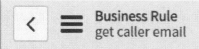

Business Rule
get caller email

A business rule is a server-side script that runs when a record is displa form fields when the specified conditions are met. More Info

Name	get caller email
Table	Incident [incident] ▼

When to run	Actions	Advanced

Specify whether the business rule should run on **Insert** or **Update**. Us

When	display ▼
Order	100
Filter Conditions	Add Filter Condition Add "OR" Clause
	-- choose field -- ▼

Under advanced it has this simple code to put the mail address of the current logged in user.

```
(function executeRule(current, previous /*null when
async*/) {

        var currentUser = gs.getUser();
        g_scratchpad.email = currentUser.getEmail();

    })(current, previous);
```

Then we can use the scratchpad in a client script to get the data and perhaps put it in a field. In this example we just put in short description to show that it works.

```
function onChange(control, oldValue, newValue, isLoading,
isTemplate) {
        if (isLoading || newValue === '') {
            return;
        }
    g_form.setValue('short_description', g_scratchpad.email);
    }
```

Now after you have been working for a while with the instance or perhaps take over an existing instance, you want to see what information is stored in the scratchpad for a specific record when it shows up in a form. You can of course go through all the **Display Business Rules** or you can just run a few lines of code in the **JavaScript Executor** I mentioned earlier, and it will show you all the information that is stored in the **g_scratchpad.** There might even be some other parameters that comes with the Baseline configuration. So, if you open up the editor and run this code, you should get a nice formatted InfoMessage on the screen.

```
var allScratchpadValues = '';


Object.getOwnPropertyNames(g_scratchpad).forEach(function(val
,idx, array){

        allScratchpadValues += val + " : " + g_scratchpad[val]
+ '<br><br>';
    });

    g_form.addInfoMessage(allScratchpadValues);
```

Using GlideAjax

We have just talked about how to use the g_scratchpad to give client-side coding more data to use than what is visible on the form. We also covered what are the pros and cons when you compare **g_scratchpad** and making a **GlideAjax** call. Let's see how we setup a GlideAjax call in a client script. And keep in mind that with the Madrid release, you might be doing a call for an **Action or Flow** instead. In this example we want to setup so that when a user is selecting a Configuration Item on the incident record, it should do a server call, get the support group of that Configuration Item and then insert that in the Assignment group field on the incident form. Since the requirement is that this should be done before the save, **Assignment Rules** aren't possible to use.

First, we need to set up the Script Include to get us this information. I have created a Script Include called acmeClientScriptUtil and checked the **Client Callable** field. In the script I have the following code:

```
var acmeClientScriptUtil = Class.create();
acmeClientScriptUtil.prototype =
Object.extendsObject(AbstractAjaxProcessor, {
/**
 * Gets the sys_id from the GlideAjax call and gets the
support group.
 *
 * @param {string} sys_id - sys_id of the record that is
sent through the GlideAjax call.
 * @return {JSON} a object containing both the value and
displayValue of the support group.
 */
    getSupportGrp: function(ci_sysid) {

        var ci = this.getParameter('syspam_ci_sysid')?
this.getParameter('syspam_ci_sysid') : ci_sysid;
        var returnGrp = {};
        var getCI = new GlideRecord('cmdb_ci');
        getCI.get(ci);

        if(getCI.support_group){
            returnGrp.value =
getCI.getValue('support_group');
            returnGrp.displayValue =
getCI.getDisplayValue('support_group');

        return JSON.stringify(returnGrp);
```

```
        }
        else
            return;

    },

    type: 'acmeClientScriptUtil'
});
```

Two things that I want to point out in the script are that I'm sending back both the value (sys_id) and the display value (name) of the group that I want to use. This is to stop ServiceNow from another server call when I set the value but more about it soon. The other thing is that you might notice that I have put a parameter in the function as well. This isn't needed when doing **GlideAjax** calls since you will get that through the specific parameter in the call, but by doing that, I can use this function on the server-side code as well.

Now that I have made the Script Include, let's configure the Client Script to do the GlideAjax call. For that I have made an **onChange Client Script** on the Configuration Item field.

```
/**
 * An example of GlideAjax to get the support group of the
CI and return it as a JSON with both the value and
DisplayValue.
 * Then it's uses that data to set the assignment group.
 * onChange Client Script which runs on the Incident
Table on the field Configuration Item (cmdb_ci).

*/

function onChange(control, oldValue, newValue, isLoading,
isTemplate) {
    if (isLoading || newValue === '') {
        return;
    }

    var ga = new GlideAjax('acmeClientScriptUtil');
    ga.addParam('sysparm_name', 'getSupportGrp');
    ga.addParam('syspam_ci_sysid', newValue);

    ga.getXML(assignGrp);

    function assignGrp(response){
```

```
            var answer =
JSON.parse(response.responseXML.documentElement.getAttribute(
"answer"));
            if(answer){
                g_form.setValue('assignment_group',
answer.value, answer.displayValue);
            }
        }
    }
```

Here I call the Script Include, send with the new CI value as a parameter and does an asynchronous call to get the information back. If you don't do the asynchronous version of GlideAjax, the user can't do anything while we wait for the answer, which might end up with users complaining about ServiceNow being slow. When it's returned, I set the **assignment_group** field. As you can see, I use three parameters with the setValue function. You normally might only see the two first ones which is **field** and **value**. The last one is optional, but it contains the display value of the field. If you don't set this on a reference field, but only the sys_id, servicenow will automatically do a Server call to find out what **display value** that sys_id has. Now, you can set any display value you want, since if there is, ServiceNow doesn't validate it. But after you save, it will display the correct value..

Using GlideAjax in onSubmit Client Scripts

Normally it's best practice to always use asynchronous GlideAjax calls in Client Scripts to improve the user experience and let the user keep working until we get the response back from the server. This is done through the **.getXML()** method. Now when it comes to onSubmit, it's not recommended to do it. onSubmit is often used to verify data and abort if something is missing or not correct. In some cases, it's needed to get some fresh data from the server, and we do that through GlideAjax. If we do this asynchronous, it means that it will send the request to the server, but while we wait for the response the rest of the code/functions will run. This means that unless there are a lot of onSubmit scripts the record will be saved in the database before the response comes back with perhaps information that makes you want to stop the save but it's too late. For this you will need to use a synchronous GlideAjax call, and you can do this with **.getXMLWait()**.

Apply a template

Sometimes you want to apply a template on a form by scripting. This can be done with the function **applyTemplate(sys_id)**. What you need is the sys_id of the template you want to apply. Here is a simple example of it in use.

```
function onChange(control, oldValue, newValue, isLoading,
isTemplate) {
    if (isLoading || newValue === '') {
        return;
    }
    applyTemplate('acd87481d7930200f2d224837e6103f3');
}
```

What is good to know is that the user needs to have write access to the fields you want to fill in with the template. There is of course also an option to have a hidden "template field" on the form filled in with the template you want to use and then just get the value from that field and use it in the function. I have also noticed that it's possible to use this function in a **Display Business Rule** to set some values before the user actually sees the form, but never ended up in a requirement to use it. But it might come in handy for some requirements. Just be careful and test it before applying it to your production instance.

Get all information in XML format

In the beginning I had no idea how to check what values a field had that wasn't showing on a form. So, what I did was a lot of work with the form layout. I added the fields that I wanted to check the information in and afterwards I removed them from the form again. Now this way was time consuming and I was hoping to find another way to do this. And of course, there is. Before I get the xml part, I ended up having a very personalized list view, which you can understand isn't the best way either, but at least it didn't land in an update set or affect other users than me.

With UI Action "show XML":

While watching a YouTube video, I suddenly saw the use of "Show XML" that you have as a context menu like this:

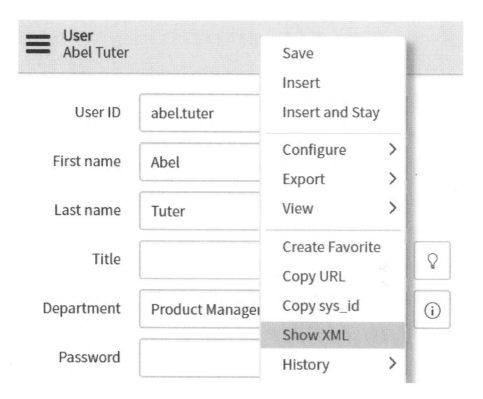

So, by right clicking and showing this you get a popup window with the xml payload with all the fields for this specific record; and they don't need to be in the form layout to show up, it shows everything. It even shows both the display value and the value of a reference field.

This XML file does not appear to have any style information associated with it. The document tree is shown below.

```
▼<xml>
  ▼<sys_user>
     <active>true</active>
     <avatar>063e383837303100042106710ce41f13b</avatar>
     <building/>
     <calendar_integration>1</calendar_integration>
     <city/>
     <company display_value="ACME South
     America">227cdfb03710200044e0bfc8bcbe5d6b</company>
     <cost_center
     display_value="Engineering">d9d07bddc0a80a647cf932056ed24(
     <country/>
     <date_format/>
     <default_perspective/>
     <department display_value="Product
     Management">9a7ed3f03710200044e0bfc8bcbe5db7</department>
     <edu_status>faculty</edu_status>
```

The downside with the "Show XML" is that the popup window will disappear the moment you click outside the window. This makes it impossible to have the window open while you click somewhere else or just want to check on another record. Solution in this case would be just to select everything in the windows and copy and paste it somewhere else for later use.

Now of course there is another way to get the xml payload and the ability to have two windows with two difference payloads as well.

Using the &XML-parameter on URI

There is a couple of parameters you can use on the URIs in ServiceNow and &XML is one of them. By adding the &XML to an existing URI, instead of giving you the record form it will give you the exact same payload as you had in the popup window with the example above but this one will stay in the browser tab and you can throw up as many tabs as you want for this.

One thing that is important is that you have to have the correct URI to get it to work. If you go to a form through the UI that looks something like this:

Here you can see that the URI has a path that starts with /nav_to.do?uri=%2Fincident.do%3Fsys_id. Here the &XML won't work, since it still thinks that the tablename is nav_to and not incident. So, we need to have a form in a browser without the navigator module or the header menu to get this to work.

One way to do to get this is to right-click on the information icon on the list and open in a new tab. Then you will see that the path starts with "/incident.do?sys_id=" which will be better. You can also see that both the banner frame and navigator are gone.

Now you can just add &XML to the end of the URI and you will get a nice wrap up of the xml-file of this record. Just like the popup, but you can open multiple records in different tabs and compare.

This XML file does not appear to have any style information associated with it. The

```xml
▼<xml>
  ▼<incident>
      <actions_taken/>
      <active>true</active>
      <activity_due/>
      <additional_assignee_list/>
      <approval>not requested</approval>
      <approval_history/>
      <approval_set/>
      <assigned_to/>
      <assignment_group/>
      <business_duration/>
```

The use of different views

Sometimes you want to have different fields on the form depending on different choices that has been made. A good example might be Change form, where depending on it's a Normal-, Standard or emergency change you want to have different fields. Now, putting them all in one form will not be the best choice, since then the user will always see fields that isn't needed and makes it harder for the user to be efficient. And for this you might build 3 different views, one for each change type.

To get the user to have the correct view, you can then for example use view rules or the URI parameter "sysparm_view".

View rules

If you build a view rule like this, with just conditions and filling in the view-field, it will work to test it as an admin.

But if you check advanced and do some scripting, suddenly this view rule won't run when you are logged in as admin, but it will work for a user without the admin role. So always try to remember to test with a user with the correct credentials, even if you think it should affect your admin account as well.

Sysparm view

Adding sysparm_view="view_name" will work as well. For example, "/incident.do?sys_id=cd7a94ff0a0006d40024722acc996dbe&sysparm_view=Metric s". But this is also ignored by the admin user but will apply to the normal users. And if you don't want the user to be able to change the view, adding "**&sysparm_view_forced=true**" will remove the view choice from the context menu here:

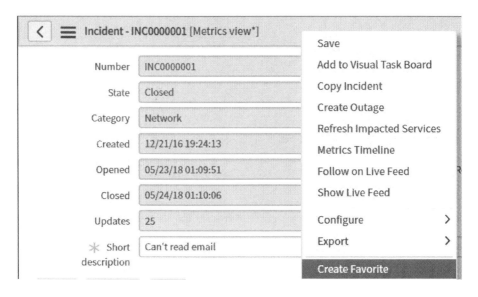

Here you can see that the **View** choice is gone from the list and the view name in the banner has gotten a * indicating that it's forced on and can't be changed.

User preference hides information on the form

Now there is a few personal settings a user can do that changes how the forms looks like. First setting is the one called **Compact the user interface**.

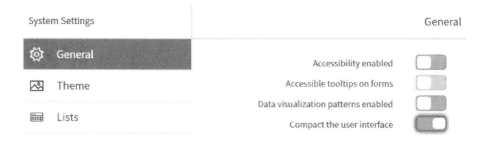

If this is selected it will remove the table name from the form header. This is how it looks when it's turned off:

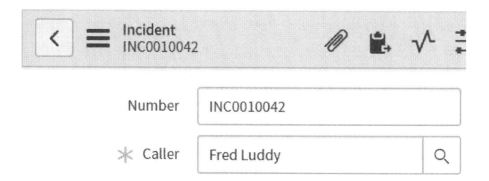

And if I activate it, you can see the table name disappear.

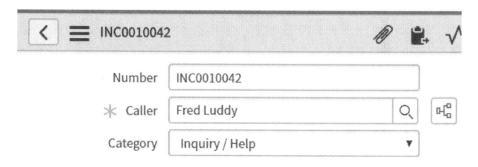

Another thing that you user can do in the Baseline installation is to personalize the form and choose which fields they want to see or not. This is done by pressing this icon and a dropdown will show.

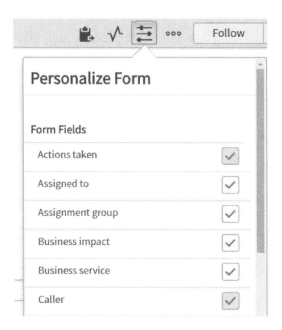

They can't remove mandatory fields which are grey in the picture above or add fields that isn't on the form from the start of the specific view. What is good to know is that even if they have removed a field or two, if you as an admin add a new field it will show up on the form. It doesn't work like how personalize list does where if you do any changes, the changes to the global view isn't applied.

Get variables visible on catalog tasks

Sometimes you want to be able to see the **variables** on the Requested Item on the Catalog Tasks that are being created through the Workflow/Flow. It's quite simple to get this to work as long as you know where to look to configure it. There are basically two steps you need to do and then you are all setup and ready to rock and roll. First out is to make sure the **Variable Editor** is on the Catalog Task form. Go to a Catalog Task record and go into the **Context menu -> Configure -> Form Layout**. Make sure you have the Variable Editor where you want it.

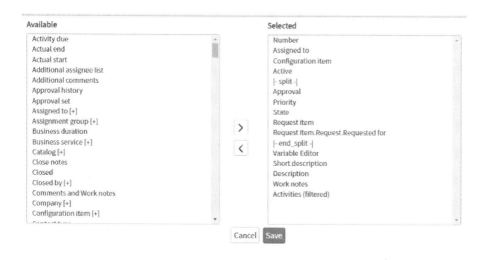

After that you will need to go into the workflows/flows which has the tasks where you want to show the variables.

For workflows you need to **Checkout** the workflow and edit the task activity that you want to show the variables on. Then you scroll down to the bottom where you find the **Add variables.** There you will see all variables from all the items that is linked to this workflow. Move over all the variables you want to see on the Catalog Task. In this case I have moved over everything.

At the moment, I can't see how to do this in a Flow, since there you need to specify which item you want to get the variables from. That limits down the flow choice if this is something you really need. But Flows are still moving fast in development and I don't doubt we will see functionality for this soon as well.

Different related lists

When you look at related lists for a table you might notice that there are two kind of rows in the slushbucket. It might look like this:

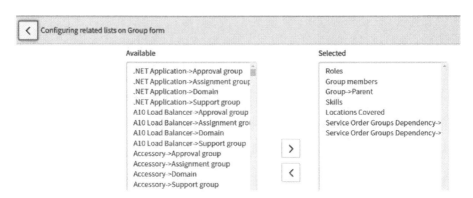

Here you can see that you have e.g. **Group-> Parent** and you have e.g. **Group members** without any `->`. Why are they different? Here is the answer.

- **Group -> Parent:** This means that it shows records in the **Group** table where the current record is in the **Parent** field which is a reference field to the group table. This is an one-to-many relationship. There can only be one value in the **Parent** field, but there can be many records with the same value in the **Parent** field.

- **Group members:** This means that it shows all the records in the **Group members** table where the current record is in either the **From table-** or **To table-field.** This is a many-to-many table that handles the relationship between groups and members.

Create your custom related list

Sometimes you get the requirement to add a related list. First of all, double check if it already exists. This since there a lot of baseline related lists just sitting there waiting to be used and some of them might match your requirement. But let's say it doesn't. Your requirement is that on the problem form, you can see all incidents that are related to the specific problem. But you have no clue if that incident has any children and even if there is only one incident in the related list, it may have 100+ child incidents connected. When it comes to this requirement, there are other options as well, like the **Related incidents** counter that exists in the problem. This also counts like the Baseline related list and gives the wrong impression. But in this example, we aren't going to fix that as well, just show the whole picture with a related list.

First thing we need to do is to create our related list and that is done through **System Definition -> Relationships**. Click **New** and set the fields to the following:

Here you can see we have defined that this related list to show on the **Problem** table and query records from the **Incident** table..

Now we are going to add the code to how to find the incidents we want. When we create the code, we have access to both **Current** and **Parent**. What is important to remember is that **Parent** is the record that you are looking on in the form. **Current** is the records that will show up in the list.

```
(function refineQuery(current, parent) {

    //Get all incidents that are connected to a parent
    var getAllParentInc = new GlideRecord('incident');
    getAllParentInc.addQuery('problem_id',
parent.getUniqueValue());
    getAllParentInc.addActiveQuery();
    getAllParentInc.query();

    var allParentInc = [];//Prepare an array to save the
sys_ids

    while (getAllParentInc.next()){
        //Push in all sys_ids of incidents that are
connected to a parent

    allParentInc.push(getAllParentInc.getUniqueValue());
    }
    //Add to the query that either the incident has parent
problem or connected to a parent incident which has a problem
connected
```

```
    current.addQuery('problem_id',
parent.getUniqueValue()).addOrCondition('parent_incident',
'IN', allParentInc);

    })(current, parent);
```

In this code you can see that I first get all active incidents that are connected to a problem and pushes their sys_id's into an array. After that I add to the query for list of records that either the incident should be related to this specific problem (**Parent**) or the incident is connected to a parent incident which is related to this problem.

In my test instance this gives me a list that looks like this where I also added the fields **Parent Incident** and **Problem** so you can see the result and that I get the children as well.

	Number ▼	Parent Incident	Problem	Opened
	INC0010043		PRB0000001	12/28/18 19:14:35
	INC0010042	INC0010043		12/21/18 16:13:11
	INC0010040	INC0010043		12/19/18 15:49:06
	INC0000019		PRB0000001	05/12/18 01:44:39

Incidents (2) | Problem Tasks | Outages | Security Incidents | All parent & Child incidents (4)

All parent & Child incidents — New — Go to — Number ▼ — Search

Incidents

HOMEPAGES

Homepages have been around for quite some time and are basically used to give the users a good overview of what is happening through showing reports and gauges on a single page. There are a few good Baseline homepages that gives you a good overview of what you can do with it. Dashboards have come a long way as well and are a newer functionality where you can do a bit more advanced and better looking UI.

There isn't so much to say about homepages, but one thing that I stumbled over was the use of lists in a homepage. When doing this, it is using the user preference for the number of rows to view, making the homepage experience very bad in most of the cases. This can easily make a homepage suddenly 2-3 pages long and the user needs to scroll down to see the reports at the bottom. As you can see here, the top report takes up the whole page. Leaving the user to scroll down to see the rest.

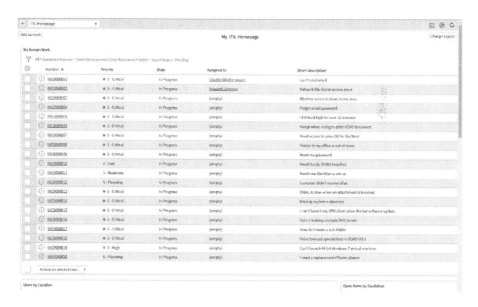

Now what you can do is set a specific number of rows on this report alone. Go to **Homepage Admin -> Pages** and click on the homepage you want to edit. Now comes the hardest part which is to find the correct dropzone that you want to change. You find them in the related list **Portal**. If you don't know which on you want to do the change, click on the arrow on the left to expand the information and look at the title. There you get the information about which dropzone you are looking at. You might need to hover the mouse over the title to get the whole title.

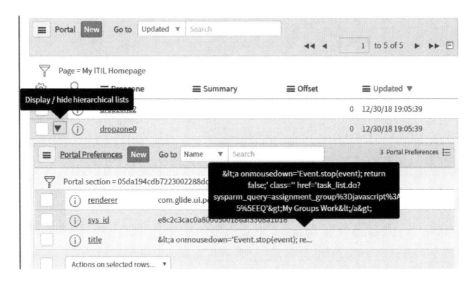

In this case you can see **My Groups Work** there in the popup. Now we are adding a new **Portal Preference** that is called **sysparm_rows_per_page** and give it the value of 5 since we only want to show 5 rows. Then it should look like this:

Now if I go back to the homepage, you can see that I only have 5 rows per page now and the other reports below are actually showing up without needing to scroll down.

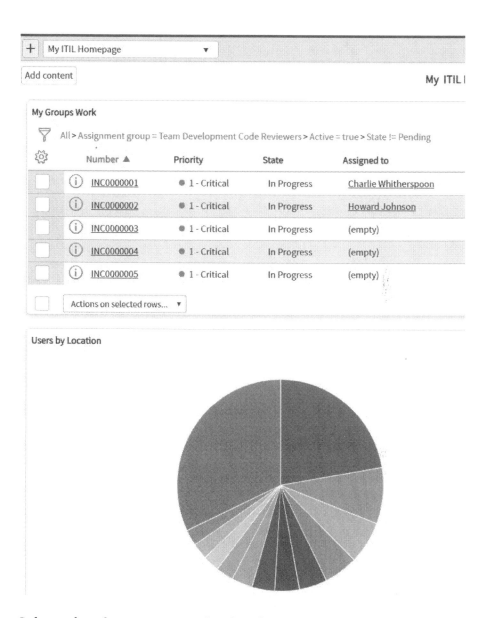

Before we leave homepages, remember that after you have done changes, they aren't default saved into your update set. To have homepages saved into the update set you need to **Unload** the hompage. This is done at **Homepage Admin -> Pages** and then you right-click on the record you want to save to the update set and the option of **Unload Portal Page** appears..

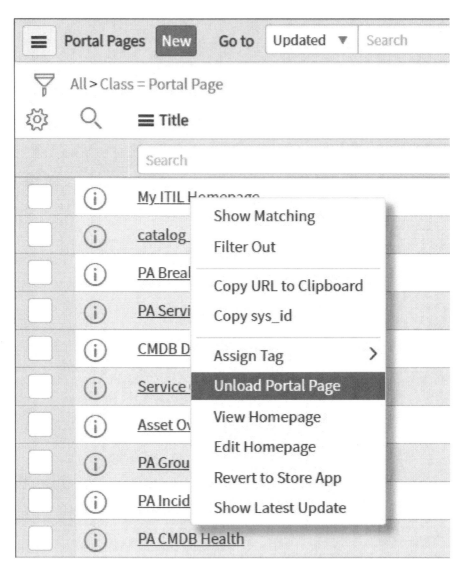

Selecting it will move your changes into the update set. Remember that the reports etc. that you use on the homepage doesn't get saved into the update set when doing this, they need to be added to it the normal way.

NOTIFICATIONS

Notifications have always been around and most of us connect notifications with emails. But it's not just emails anymore. There are of course also SMS and push-messages. Say what you want about the Native app, but it hasn't been used that much. Now with the Madrid release the app get a total refresh. Both the end user, but also for the ones building/configuring it. I hope this Madrid is the release where we take another step into using the app and e.g. push-message. After all, we all want to step away from email. Then in the newer releases we are getting other channels as well. For example, you can integrate and send messages through **MicroSoft Teams** and **Slack** with Baseline integrations.

When it comes to notifications, there are multiple ways of triggering and sending them. I recommend trying to keep all notifications in one place. I try to keep all possible notifications within the notifications at **System Notification -> Email ->Notifications**. What I'm talking about is e.g. in Workflows where you can do a notification activity and send the email through it. I feel doing this makes it a lot harder when trouble shooting etc. since these notifications don't show up under the module I mention above. Instead in Workflows I recommend using an event activity and then trigger the notification on that specific event. But this is just a personal setup I have.

Weights

To see the **Weight** field you need to go to **Advanced view** and look under the **When to send** section.

Weight is used to help stop the user from being spammed with emails. If a change to a record is triggering multiple notifications, weight is used to decide which notification is going to be sent. The normal case is that if multiple notifications are being triggered, all notifications create a record in the **Email (sys_email)** table. But the only notification that is being sent is the one with the highest value in weight. The rest of the records will be moved into the **Skipped** mailbox and never sent. Like many other things, there is an exception as well. If you set the value to 0 on a notification, it will always be sent. This also applies if you have multiple notifications triggered with value 0. All of them will be sent. If there is one with 0 that has been triggered, then the notification with the highest value won't be sent.

Send to event creator

Another field that is good to know and understand is the **Send to event creator**. Here you also need to click on **Advanced view** and go to the section **Who will receive**.

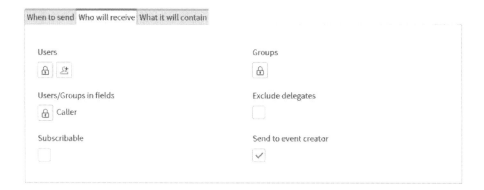

With this, you can control if the user triggering the notification should get the notification if they are in any of the Who will receive fields. For example, you have a notification that goes to the assigned to if someone assign a task to a specific person. Then the user in the assigned to field will get the notification. If I assign a task to myself, I obviously don't want the mail, so I keep this field unchecked. But if I create an incident with myself as caller, I probably still want to have the email confirming the creating of the ticket with the information. In this case I make sure the field is checked.

Mandatory notification

It's possible for a user to go into their notification setting and turn of any notification they want. But sometimes you have a very important notification that you don't want the user to be able to turn off by accident. I have examples where a fulfiller had accidentally turned off the notification when an end user leaves a comment in an incident. This resulted in that they sat waiting for the end user to come back for a couple of hours before noticing that the end user wrote a comment 15 minutes after the fulfiller asked the question.

There is a field to make a notification mandatory, but it isn't on the Baseline form. So just either make the field visible on the list or on the form like this to take use of the functionality.

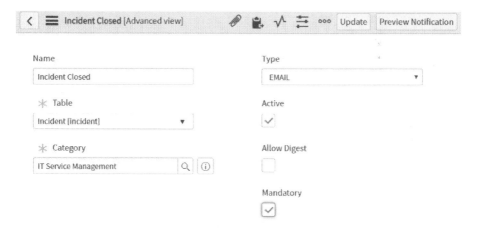

After saving a notification record with this field checked, it's no longer possible to turn off that notification anymore.

Notification Email Scripts

Mail script is a good way of reusing code in notifications. You can in a body use **<mail_script>** & **</mail_script>** to write code to make the information you want appear in the notification. Now if you want to reuse the code, mail scripts are a nice way to do it. The biggest difference between this and a template is that you can easily add multiple mail scripts in one notification while a template takes cares of the whole deal (and can of course have mail scripts in it). So, depending on your requirements, you might use templates as well sometimes.

One thing that is common is that when someone writes an additional comment, a notification goes out to the end user with the comment. Baseline, you will also get a date and who wrote the comment. This is when you use the normal ${comments} in the notification.

INC0000027 - Please remove the latest hotfix from my PC

Comments:

2018-03-19 22:31:50 CET - System Administrator   Additional comments
Comment copied from Parent Incident: test5

The main issues here are:

- It doesn't look good. The whole layout isn't so eye catching with information that you might not want either.

- Having information like date stamp and "additional comments" are things you really would like to avoid and don't really have any meaning since the notification was sent when the comment was written, and the end user has no idea what additional comments are.

- Last thing is having the user who wrote the comment visible for the end user. In some cases, it doesn't matter, but some companies don't want to show who the assignee is for the end user. It might be because of end users starting to call directly to the assignee etc.

To avoid these issues and get a better looking comment, you can do a mail script with the following example code. It's a bit longer since we can't use the getJournalEntry() since it will give us all the stuff that we want to remove.

```
var journal = new GlideRecord("sys_journal_field");
journal.addQuery("name", current.getTableName());
```

```
journal.addQuery("element", "comments");
journal.addQuery("element_id", current.getUniqueValue());
journal.orderByDesc("sys_created_on");
journal.setLimit(1);//can be changes if you want more that
the latest comment
journal.query();

if (journal.next())
template.print(journal.getValue("value"));
```

Now, I have noticed that in some occasions the new line is not being adhered and you get the whole comment in a big wall of text. To fix this, you need to check the field **Newlines to HTML** on the mail script.

Default turned off notifications

You don't want to spam the user with notifications and one way of limiting it is with **Subscribable**.

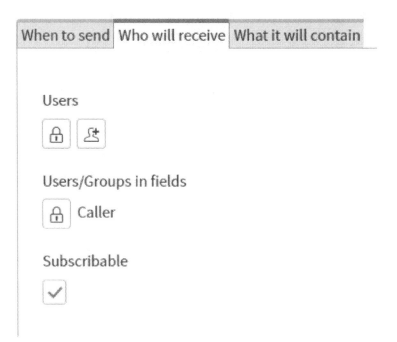

This functionality is activated through the plugin **Subscriptions 2.0**. Normally this is already activated on your instance, but if you have a really old instance you might need to activate the plugin. Now the users can go and subscribe on the notification if they want to have that active. All subscriptions are saved in the table **Notification Subscription (sys_notif_subscription)**.

USEFUL APPLICATIONS / PLUGINS

In this section, we have those plugins I found which might not be so well documented or something that everyone is talking about. But still they might be very useful and having functionality that people like or are requesting. I have also seen this functionality being developed from scratch since the people didn't know it existed in the Baseline configuration. One thing to notice about plugins is that the UI for it has changed in the Madrid release. Before it looked like a normal list view and now this is how it looks in Madrid:

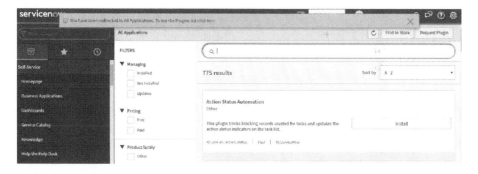

Now you can filter on paid or free plugins. Just keep in mind that it doesn't know what licenses you have bought, so even if it says **Paid** it still might mean that you can activate it without any extra costs. But like always, contact your ServiceNow representative if you are not sure if the plugin is included in the licenses you already have, or you need to get others. You can still click on the **Click here** in the message to go to the old list view if you want.

Templated Snippets

Templated snippets is a plugin/functionality that has been popping up in the HR area and where ServiceNow is mention it as a functionality. After the plugin has been activated, you can see it's got its own scoped application called **Templated Snippets**.

So, what is template snippets? It helps handle repetitive responses which they use in the communication with the end users. In ServiceNow you might find a row or two about this for the HR agents, but I can see the IT Service Desk using it as well. When I sat in the first line, we had these responses saved in notepad and with copy&paste it was used frequently. With this application, you can choose your response and then just click to get it into the clipboard and easily paste into for example close notes or additional comments.

Also worth mentioning is that this feature seems to only work on tables extended from task (or a table that has its base table from task). Good to know when creating your own custom tables that might want to have this feature.

Remember to not mix this with the "normal" templates that exists. I would rather have seen this to be called something like "response templates" instead. Just to try to keep the confusion at the lowest level.

Here is an example how it looks like on the incident table:

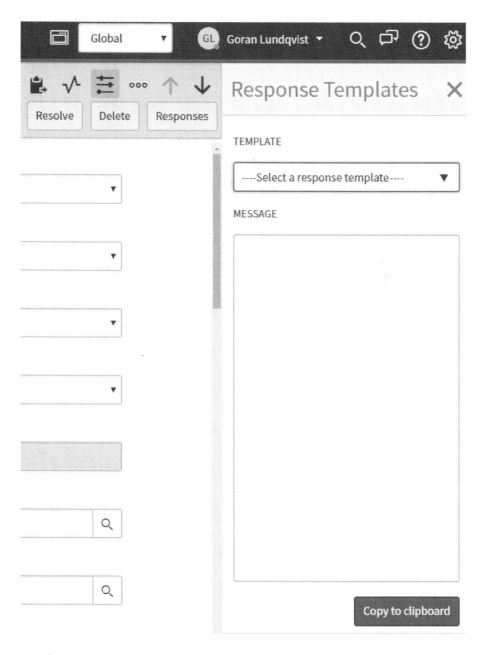

It's very simple to get this up and running and here is how to do it. First you need to activate the plugin **Templated Snippets (com.sn_templated_snip)**.

1 results for "templated sn"

Templated Snippets
Human Resources Management

Activated with Human Resources Scoped App: Core [com.sn_hr_core].
Creates pre-defined and reusable responses that can be added to any ...

ID: com.sn_templated_snip | Free | by ServiceNow

After that a few things have been created that we are going to look at.

Admin page

You can find an **Administration page** under **System Definition -> Response Template Configuration**. This module will give you a list of the responses(templates) that have been created.

This will give you a list over the available response templates you have.

Now, let's look at what fields there are available for us and what we can do.

In this example you can see there are mainly 4 fields.

- **Name:** Contains the name the user will see in the dropdown field when choosing a response.

- **Table:** This defines on what table the response is for. This also will be used for the field assistant that are on the right. Where you can easily find and use the field values in your template body.

- **Condition:** At the bottom you can see a normal condition field. This is used to be able to decide when the specific response template is going to visible in the dropdown. A good feature to make sure that the user only sees responses that are useful to the specific task they are working on.

- **Template body:** This holds the text. Can say it's pretty much the same as the body field on notifications and you can use the field assistant on the right to select different fields that are on the table. Worth noticing is that there also is a UI Action "Insert Current Date" which is used to have the current date (when the response is used) in the text itself which might come in handy.

When you have created your template, it will then show up in the dropdown if the conditions match and the user can copy and paste in the response in additional comments, etc. By doing that it will take the field values and put that into the response for a more dynamic personal response.

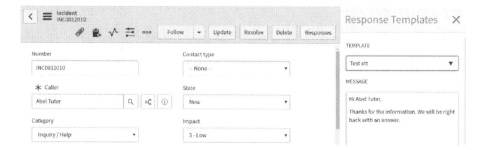

Service Desk Call

Service Desk Call is a small plugin that has been around for quite some time. But Service Desk Call can be very useful to help the 1st line decide what the call should become. Should it be an incident, change and so on. Before deciding this, they can log it as a call and then afterwards transfer to the correct process. This can also be used to log e.g. Wrong Number for statistics.

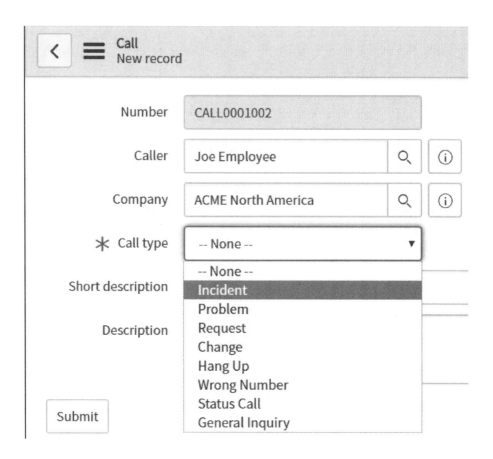

This can also be used to handle incoming mail that isn't connected to any existing task. Since it can be hard to the end user to know what type of task their request/problem should become. The solution might be to have incoming mail create a call instead and then let the 1st line decide and transfer the call to the correct type.

Interaction Logging, Routing and Queueing

This is like the newer version of Service Desk Call. I have seen Baseline usage of this for example within the Customer Service Management Application. There are some differences between this, and Service Desk Call and one important missing functionality is when you associate it with a task, nothing from the interaction record is auto filling the task. I'm thinking e.g. caller or short description. But I don't see that being such a big trouble to configure yourself until it's there at Baseline level. Interactions also consider different queues. Meaning with having interactions is to have one flexible way of communicating with the users no matter which process/task you are working with.

Reminder

Now, this isn't a plugin, it's active from the start and belongs to the NOW Platform. This table/application can be used to generate reminders for users on records from task-table or tables extended from it. For example, the incident table can use this to send reminders at a specific time. It's a very simple functionality but appreciated by the users.

Here you can see how you define which task the reminder is connected to (**Task**), who should receive the reminder (**User**), how long before the deadline (**Remind me**) and which field holds the deadline (**Before**). In this case an email will be sent that looks like this:

Preview Email

You requested a reminder in regards to INC0012010.
Link: LINK
Notes: just for testing

Performance Analytics and Reporting – Service Portal Widgets

No clue why this is not active from the start or why it is mixed together with Performance Analytics. I'm guessing that it's the people from the PA application that made this and that's why it has the name. This is a very small plugin which only contains two widgets and the files they use e.g. CSS Includes and JS Includes. But it's free to use and it also works for normal reports as well, not only Performance Analytics reports. I've seen a lot of custom solutions for showing reports on the portal and these Baseline widget might not cover them all, but most of them and it's a good start.

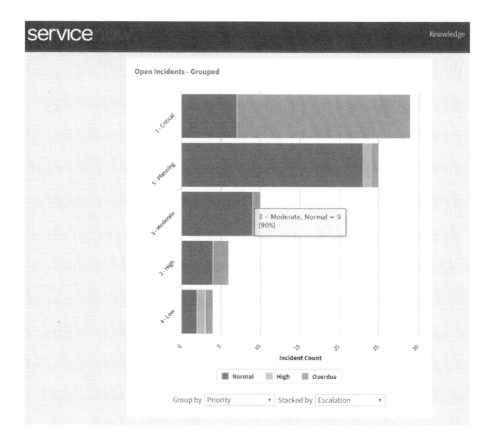

Open Incidents - Grouped

AGENT WORKSPACE

Agent Workspace showed up in London as a Limited Access. This basically means that just a few customers gets access to it. I would personally compare this to beta testing. And then in the Madrid release it became General Access which pretty much means that it's available for everyone. This is a whole new UI which has both its pros and cons. Right now, it's made for the first tier agents and it's important to understand that as it is right now in Madrid release, not all users should use this interface. They can of course, but there might be missing functionality that e.g. exists within UI16. I had the privilege to work with Agent Workspace in the London release and I have gathered here all my experience and thoughts about it. I will not go deep into each functionality and how to configure it. It's very easy to configure, there is also a Guided Tour for setting it up which I recommend using. I will focus on what small things I found that exists or is missing. My personal summary of **Agent Workspace** is that I like it a lot. And I think that this will be standard UI in a few releases.

General

Agent Workspace has its own application. So just go here to find all the things you need. When you want to reach the UI click on **Agent Workspace Home**.

Remember that users can choose if they want to work in this **UI** or **UI16**. Only thing differ might be some functionality that only work in one of the places. When you click on the module it will open up in a new tab.

Right now you can't do anything with this home screen. I'm guessing this will evolve into some kind of dashboard as well to give the user a good overview. But as now in Madrid, there isn't anything we can configure here. Main work will be either through the + button to create new records (which you can define) and the list view which comes here. Good to know is that when you configure which tables you can create record in you can't use wizards/interceptors. This means that e.g. like on change when you click **Create** New and then get to choose which type of change you want to create isn't possible here. Before we look into list there is another thing worth mention that will be visible the whole time. On the upper right, you have a **magnifying glass** which is the global search. Agent Workspace has their own global search which you define where and what it should search for. This UI also works with tabs and no popup or so. This means that tabs will show up like this:

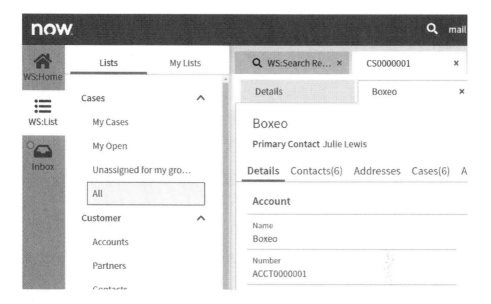

Here I first have a tab for my search, next to it is a case which is open in the **Details** tab. On the form I have clicked on the "i" on the reference field of the account **Boxeo**. Then instead of a popup, that record will come as a tab to the right of the details tab.

There is a lot of tabs and it takes some time to get used to it, but after that it's real nice.

Lists

Back to lists which looks like this when I click on the list icon to the left.

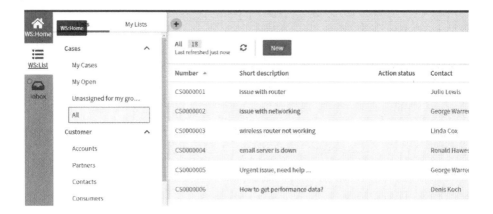

You as admin or users with the role **workspace_list_admin** can configure which modules is going to show up here. New compared to old lists is that you can define who can see it with both roles and groups. Another nice thing here is that you for each list (module) you define which columns should be visible. I really like this compared to the old list view where you either had to have multiple views or have the same columns on all lists for a table. Users can also easy create their own lists if they want. Worth mention is that **field styles** only works on the lists. They do not apply on fields in a form and it's only the **background color** you can change which then becomes a **colored dot** like you might have seen in the old list view and e.g. priority on incidents.

Form

First thing that comes into mind is that you should have the same mindset here as on the Service Portal. Nothing with Jelly works here and client scripts needs to be marked as **Mobile/Service Portal** or **All** to run on these forms.

One thing that you might stumble over fast is that the record is read only with a message like this:

This form has not been configured for Workspace. To edit the form, select a different type of record, or contact your administrator.

This will happen if the table doesn't have a view called **Workspace, workspace_itil** or **Workspace_csm**. If it doesn't have it, this error will show and the form will be read only. Easy solved by just created a view with the fields you want to have on it. Reason for the three roles is that depending on what role the user has, it will use more specific view. E.g. a user with the role **sn_esm_agent** will use the view **workspace_csm** if both **workspace_csm** and **workspace** views exist. While if they have the role **itil** the **workspace_itil** view will take precedence over the **Workspace** view. But as long as there is at least a **Workspace** view it will not be read only.

There been a few changes on where things are on the form. One of the biggest change is that the related lists has been moved to almost the top. Here you can see related lists lining up to the right after **Details**. Remember that if you want to be able to edit records in related lists, those tables also need the **Workspace** view or they will be read only.

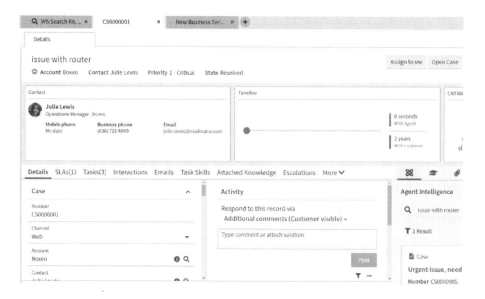

Attachments has also been move and is harder to see. If you look at the picture above you might see a little paperclip. That is where you need to click to see if there is any attachments. Here is a closer look:

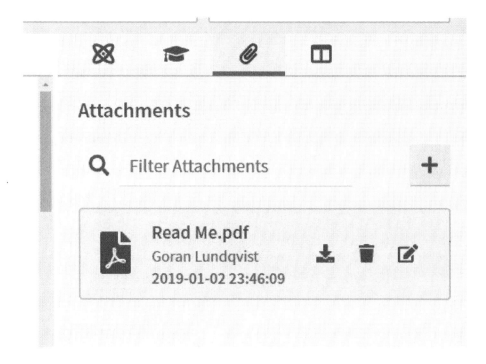

Hopefully there can be some kind of indicator like a counter or similar on the right side of the paperclip so the user doesn't need to click on it to see if there is any attachment or not.

There is also a few things that doesn't work in Workspace and one of them is **Presence**. The functionality where you can see who else is looking at the record, if someone else changes something and save the record would automatically update without needed to refresh the page. This doesn't work yet in Workspace and potentially this means that two users can overwrite each other's changes.

I mention the plugin **Templated snippets** earlier in this book and that doesn't work with Workspace either. That only works with UI16.

UI Macro doesn't work either. And it's pretty simple since it's Jelly and it doesn't work in the Service Portal and not in Agent Workspace. There might be 3:rd party applications etc. that has a nice icon besides the field on UI16, which will not then work in **Workspace.**

If you are using **Tags**, then you can't see them on the form.

UI Actions

UI Actions has gotten some changes and if you have own custom UI Actions, they need to be fixed to work within the Agent Workspace. In UI16 you have both the client- and server-side code in the same field called **Script**. But if you want to have client code in the Workspace UI you will need to put that code in a specific new field. Workspace will ignore all client-side code that exists within the old **Script** field. This means that if you want to have the same client-side functionality within both **UI16** and **Workspace** you will need to have the code in two fields and needs to keep both up to date. Might even end up with different code as well. To handle the new Workspace functionality there has been created a new section on the UI Action form with a couple of new fields.

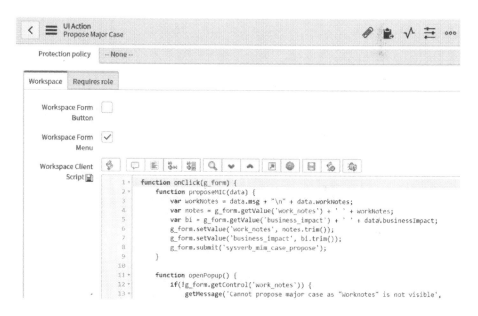

There are two checkboxes that you can use to decide where the UI Action should appear and then there is a **Workspace Client Script** field. If You don't see the new **Workspace Client Script** field, then it's probably because you haven't checked any of the two fields above the Workspace Client script field. It will not appear until you have checked at least one.

From scratch there is a **onClick** function from which you should wrap your code inside. So if you want your UI Action to work in both **UI16** and **Workspace** then the code needs to be in both Script places. Server-side code should still be in the old

Script field. One thing to notice here is that it has scrapped the old **gsftSubmit(null, g_form.getFormElement(), 'sysverb_mim_case_propose')** which saved the form and then called for the UI Action to run the server-side code. I haven't found any official documentation about that function or anyone that could actually explain what the different parameters were for, besides the last one containing the UI action's **Action name**. Now it uses **g_form.submit('sysverb_mim_case_propose')** which is a lot easier to understand and where you just need to add the **Action name**. You can do it even more dynamic by using the **g_form.getActionName()** and write use it like this **g_form.submit(g_form.getActionName())**. On the side note is that you can actually use **g_form.submit()** instead of **gsftSubmit()** in the old script field as well.

Some UI Actions are used to open up a url in a new tab. This can still be done, but depending on how you done it before, it might not work. For example the **g_navigation** API doesn't work in Agent Workspace. What you can do instead is this.

```
var win = top.window.open('http://www.coolsite.com',
'_blank');
   win.focus();
```

That will open up the site www.coolsite.com in a new tab and open that tab.

Client Script

Like mention before, to make the client script run on Agent Workspace you need to be sure that **UI type** is **Mobile / Service Portal** or **All**. If not, the script will **not** run in the workspace form. Beside that most important is that you make sure you don't use to much (rather not anything) of DOM Manipulation. With this new UI your old code with DOM Manipulation will to 99% not work and this is also one of the reason it's never recommended to go down that path if not really needed. But sometimes you need scripts that you just want to run on **UI16** or on **Agent Workspace**. Only on UI16 is easier, since you can basically just change the UI type to **Desktop** and it will only work on UI16. But having it the other way around was a bit tricker. The script will always run on both, but you can add a simple line of code to check if it's in the UI16 or Agent Workspace.

```
var env = typeof g_form.initialize === 'undefined' ?
'mobile' : 'desktop';
```

Running the code above first in your client script will give the variable **env** the value of **mobile** if it's run in Agent Workspace and the value of **desktop** if it's run in UI16. So adding that code and then do a check if you want to continue or not.

```
var env = typeof g_form.initialize === 'undefined' ?
'mobile' : 'desktop';

if (env == 'desktop')
    return;

//do your code that you want to run in the Agent Workspace
```

TIME TO TROUBLESHOOT

Troubleshooting is actually something I find enjoyable. I love getting a strange bug and having to really go outside the normal way of thinking and attacking it from different angles trying to find the solution. Of course there is a great amount of information already out there and the biggest obstacle is to find the needle in the haystack. Here is a few places I normally use when I'm out there looking for an answer. Most important to have in mind that you probably isn't alone of running into this issue or requirement. Just need to find my fellow friend and hope that they already solved it.

ServiceNow Community

URL: https://community.servicenow.com/community

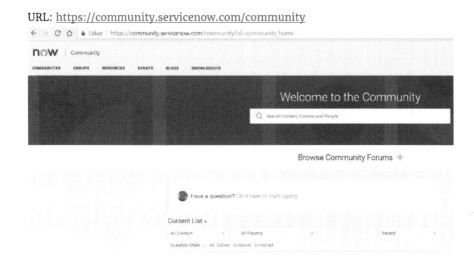

This is one of the first places I normally start searching through when I have something I can't really figure out myself. If you find a similar question which already been answered, take a look at the answer and always keep an eye on the dates then when thread was created and answered. Some solutions in there might have been the best way when the questions was asked, but now there might even be a Baseline solution for that question that isn't mention. And some solutions/suggestions might not follow what most people think of Best Practice and should be avoidable.

HI portal

URL: https://hi.service-now.com/hisp?id=hisp_search

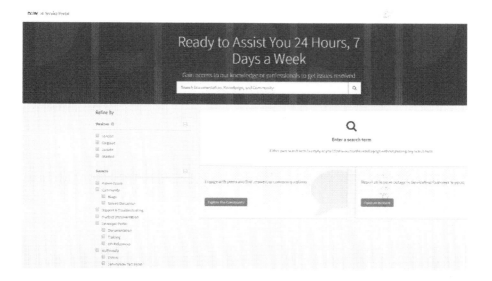

Normally I forget to go to the HI Portal and use the search functionality there. This is real useful since it searches at multiple places at the same time.

As you can see on the picture to the left it will search in multiple sources like the community, known errors, documentation site and more.

There is also an option to define which version you are interested in. Especially when we are looking for known errors this becomes a really good way of filtering.

Documentation site

URL: https://docs.servicenow.com/

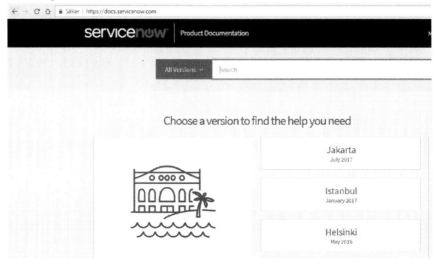

Now, even if this is covered through the HI portal, sometimes you want to dig directly into the documentation site to be able to easier click around if you not sure what exactly you are looking for or what it's called. One nice thing is that you can click into a specific release and patch level to see which bugs that patch fixed. When you have drilled down, you will come to a page that looks something like this and here you can see what it fixes:

Known error portal

URL: https://hi.service-now.com/kb_view.do?sysparm_article=KB0597477

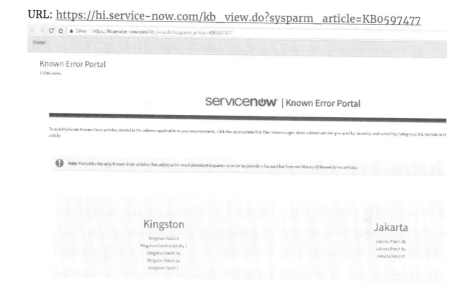

Now, as we all know and have experience with all software patches comes new errors. And this is a good place to see what new errors has come with a certain patch. Just remember that here you will only find the errors that have the biggest impact on the system. It will not show all the errors that it might have. This is also a good source to go through before doing an upgrade to a specific release/patch. Sometimes it's better to wait 1-2 patches just to avoid upgrading to a version that has a patch that have a known error that will critically impact your business.

Slack

Slack is one of many different chat/collaboration tools out there and for ServiceNow there is a real good channel called "sndevs.slack.com". If you haven't tested it, I totally recommend it. It's not an official channel from ServiceNow, but it's filled with over 4000 users and even people from ServiceNow is active in the different channels, helping people with questions. I try to spend some time here, but sadly I wish I had more time over here. There is so much good examples/solutions/ideas in these channels and you always learn new things just reading what others do and think.

Different ways of logging information

Now, there is many ways of handling logging of data in ServiceNow. Here I will just give a few tips on how you can do it and hopefully give some joy in your troubleshooting life.

When you look at the Baseline logging capabilities there are a few that I use myself. Just remember to clean out your code from unnecessary logging before you move it up the chain to production. This to keep the system logs as clean as possible in the production instance and really only log the things that you want to be able to track through the system log.

- **gs.error()**: I never use this for troubleshooting. I only use this when I actually want to put information in the system log that is relevant even on the production instance. Remember to put enough information so it's easy to trace where it's from and what the error is all about.

- **gs.info()**: One of two functions I use when troubleshooting. This ends up in the information part of the system log and I usually put a prefix on my logging so it's easy to find in the system log, since if you are multiple developers and might use many applications, the log will have a lot of records in it.

- **gs.debug()**: This is the other function I use and which I prefer to use whenever it's possible. This will fill the system log with records but will still show the information if you e.g. uses the scripts – background or Fix script. It will also show up if you are using the debug functionality.

Some might as about gs.log(), but that isn't anything I'm using anymore. ServiceNow doesn't either recommend using it either and points towards the ones I mention above.

Logging an object properties

Sometimes you are having trouble trying to get code working with an object. It might be function who returns an object, but you doesn't seem to get the correct information back. And when you try to normal gs.info() or perhaps gs.debug()to log the object to the system log you will only end up with with [object Object]:

```
var x = {};
x.name = 'Göran';
x.age = 39;
gs.info("my Object: " + x);
```

| ⓘ | 2018-05-12 21:26:25 | Information | my Object: [object Object] |

Here you have no clue what properties your object has. Many times before I knew about this other solution I created a loop to run through all the properties and list them. But there is an easy Baseline functionality that you can use and it will give you all the goodies. There is a function called JSUtil.logObject(). If you use that instead, it will give you this:

```
var x = {};
x.name = 'Göran';
x.age = 39;
JSUtil.logObject(x);
```

This will then give this line in the log files, now you get a great overview of all the properties within the object.

| ⓘ | 2018-05-12 22:31:59 | Information | Log Object
Object
name: string = Göran
age: number = 39 |

Logtail

Sometimes it easier to have access to system log in real time to see what is really happening when for example an incoming rest call is being made and you might now have the rest debug on etc. What you can do then is go to the following URI: https://YOUR_INSTANCE.service-now.com/channel.do?sysparm_channel=logtail. Then you will get to a page that looks like this:

Here you can see what going on in real time and there is also a nice checkbox to the upper right called **Auto scroll** which will let you easier go through the log and find what you are looking for.

Printed in Great Britain
by Amazon

75524917R00136